READY OR NOT
BEGINNING YOUR CAREER JOURNEY

Written and Edited by

Doug Hanvey

Adam Heeg

Beth Kreitl

Katie Lloyd

Alexa Yarnelle

Career Development Center
Arts & Sciences Career Services
Indiana University Bloomington
Patrick Donahue, Director

Career Development Center
Arts & Sciences Career Services
Indiana University Bloomington
Patrick Donahue, Director

Visit our website at IUCareers.com.

This book was designed by Derek Springston. The manuscript and layout was edited by Mary Spohn. It was printed and bound by Spectrum Press in Bloomington, Indiana.

The interior is printed on Weyerhaeuser's 70# Cougar Text Smooth, which is FSC certified and consists of 10% Post Consumer Waste. The cover is printed on Burgo's 100# Chorus Art Cover Silk, which is also FSC certified and consists of 50% Post Consumer Waste.

The text is set in Minion Pro, designed by Robert Slimbach.

The headers are set in Verlag, designed by Jonathan Hoefler and Tobias Frere-Jones.

First Edition: July 2010
10 9 8 7 6 5 4 3 2 1

ISBN: 978-0-615-37367-6

TABLE OF CONTENTS

INTRODUCTION   1

CHAPTER ONE   SETTING THE STAGE   9

Introduction   9

Motivation to Work   9

Self-Authorship as a Path to Higher Growth   11

Beliefs   15

Activities   21

Summary and Key Points   23

CHAPTER TWO   VALUES   25

Introduction   25

Different Roles, Different Values   25

Values—Subjective and Personal   26

Conflicting Values, Changing Values   27

Activities   29

Summary and Key Points   32

CHAPTER THREE   SKILLS   33

Introduction   33

Types of Skills   33

How to Identify Your Skills   35

Developing Skills   36

Activities   38

Summary and Key Points   46

CHAPTER FOUR · **INTERESTS** — **47**

Introduction — 47

The Origin of Your Interests — 48

Holland's Theory of Occupational Interests — 49

The Six Themes — 50

Your Holland Theme Code — 56

Activities — 60

Summary and Key Points — 61

CHAPTER FIVE · **PERSONALITY PREFERENCES** — **63**

Introduction — 63

Jung's Psychological Type Theory and the MBTI® Instrument — 64

Natural Preferences — 65

The Four Dichotomies — 65

Estimate Your Personality Type — 70

Exploring Type Dynamics — 71

Personality Preferences and Career Development — 75

Activities — 80

Summary and Key Points — 81

CHAPTER SIX · **MAKE THE CONNECTIONS** — **83**

Activities — 85

Summary and Key Points — 102

CHAPTER SEVEN **EXPLORING AND CHOOSING MAJORS** **103**

Introduction 103

Your Personal Career Profile in Major Research 103

Nuts and Bolts: How Academic Institutions Are Organized 104

What Majors Are Out There? 107

Researching Majors and Other Academic Programs 108

Relationship Between Major and Career 109

Activities 111

Summary and Key Points 114

CHAPTER EIGHT **DISCOVERING YOUR CAREER OPTIONS** **115**

Introduction 115

Your Personal Career Profile and Career Research 115

Career Research Resources 116

Career Research through Experiential Learning 118

Employer Research 122

Activities 125

Summary and Key Points 126

CHAPTER NINE	**MAKING DECISIONS**	**127**
	Introduction	127
	The Complexities of Decision Making	127
	A Decision-making Model	132
	Your Best-fit Approach to Making Decisions	135
	Activities	137
	Summary and Key Points	141

CHAPTER TEN	**SETTING GOALS**	**143**
	Introduction	143
	Personality and Goal Setting	144
	Levels of Goals	144
	SMART Goals	145
	Activities	148
	Summary and Key Points	151

CHAPTER ELEVEN	**MAKE YOURSELF MARKETABLE**	**153**
	Introduction	153
	Where to Begin	153
	Meeting Employers' Needs	154
	Networking	158
	Activities	159
	Summary and Key Points	160

REFERENCES		**163**

INTRODUCTION

Who am I? Why am I here? What should I study? What kind of work might I enjoy? What if I choose a major or career I don't like? What if I get stuck? Do these questions sound familiar? Choosing a major and career is very exciting, but it can be a task that causes great confusion. As you begin your college career, it is important to take steps to bring clarity and intentionality to your decision-making process. Approaching it as a massive, one-time event will add to the uncertainty, and might be overwhelming. This text presents an approach to career planning that is broken down into a manageable, step-by-step process.

A BRIEF HISTORY OF WORK

In early human societies, there were no models or theories to guide career choices. Instead, the work of hunters and gatherers was determined by gender and the needs of the community. However, according to career development author Laurence Boldt, there have been three major revolutions that have each impacted the world of work in a unique way.

The first revolution, the rise of civilization through the birth of agriculture, brought about the idea of each individual having a potential choice in the type of work they pursued (e.g., store owner, farmer, blacksmith). For the first time, work could be dedicated to something other than basic survival needs. Though there were many more options, most people's occupations were determined by what their parents had done, which was influenced by social structures such as class or caste systems.

The second major change, the industrial revolution, dramatically altered the world of work again. Occupations became much more specialized and people began relying on machines, working in factories, building cars; efficiency became the "almighty." Long hours were required of men, women, and children, giving rise to laws, labor unions, and agencies designed to protect workers. The ability to move up to higher classes became possible and was a reality for many people. Public education also helped to level the playing field and brought promise and hope to many workers and their families. As the opportunity to choose careers evolved, the field of vocational guidance began. Industrial psychologists were hired to "test and match" employees to ensure they were as productive as possible. This approach reflected the belief that both the employee and the employment options remained permanent, meaning that an employee would most likely work in the same job, for the same employer, for their entire career.

The third significant shift, the electronic revolution and globalization, is the most recent shift and has had a profound impact on the way we approach work. The competition brought about by the global market, the entrance of more women and minorities into the workforce, and the elimination and creation of jobs brought about by new information and technology have resulted in a much more volatile world of work. Job security is no longer a given; it has been replaced by the dynamic process of discovering one's passions and values and resourcefully applying those to one's work.

CAREER THEORIES

Given the complexity of our current career planning environment, it is helpful to examine some of the theories or approaches developed to guide our understanding and exploration of the process.

The theoretical constructs presented provide a framework for gaining insight into the stages and many facets of career planning. As you study these ideas, you will discover new language to conceptualize, simplify, and articulate what you already have experienced, and will continue to experience, in this exciting journey.

The Overview of Career Theories table provides broad categories of career development theories, adapted from Zunker's summaries, along with highlights of a few specific theories within each group.

Overview of Career Theories

Trait-and-Factor Theories: Matching Skills to Employment Opportunities

Parsons' Trait-and-Factor

This is one of the earliest career theories and was strongly influenced by Frank Parsons, the "Father of Career Development." The theory recommends that you assess your skills and interests and match them to career options. Many contemporary career assessments are grounded in this theory.

Person-Environment Correspondence (PEC)

This theory is unique in that it focuses on longer-range issues and examines your needs and how those are being met in your particular work environment. PEC also places a strong emphasis on work relationships and states that they can contribute significantly to satisfaction with your work.

John Holland's Typology

Holland believed that you choose your work based on your personal characteristics and significant early life activities. He developed a coding system containing six interest areas and six types of work environments and stated that when your chosen work environment matches your interests, you are most likely to be satisfied. Holland's theory has been influential and is also the underpinning for many career assessments such as the Strong Interest Inventory® instrument (to be discussed in CHAPTER 4).

Social Learning Theories: Assessing Learning and Environmental Influences

Krumboltz's Learning Theory

Krumboltz's theory concentrates on your ability to make career decisions as a result of learning. He believes that the foundation of learning happens through an interaction of your genetic talents, environment and learning experiences. The relationship of these factors results in the development of skills needed to accomplish specific tasks which Krumboltz emphasizes must be ever-changing to meet the demands of the world of work.

Cognitive Information Processing

This theory suggests that your information processing skills and problem solving are essential in the career planning process. Consequently its goals are to raise self-awareness and potential conflicting beliefs associated with the career development process to increase effectiveness in decision making and problem solving.

Social Cognitive

Social Cognitive theory has a very broad scope as it hypothesizes that all of your experiences, scenarios and events shape your career behavior in a complex, interconnected manner. The theory also proposes that self-efficacy is a significant aspect of career development and will largely impact your performance and thus the efficiency of interactions you have with all levels of your social environment.

Developmental Theories: Evaluating the Growth Process and Corresponding Tasks

Life Span

Donald Super proposed this developmental career theory which suggests that the career development process has distinct stages (adolescence through late adulthood), each one including stage-specific tasks. The life span theory underlies many other developmental theories which more accurately and clearly reflect the landscape of our current workforce.

Career Construction

Mark Savickas developed this more current theory on Super's life-stage model (described above). It focuses on empowering you to take control over your career planning through developing an interest in your future, understanding educational and occupational choices, and gaining the confidence needed to successfully pursue your options.

A WORKING MODEL OF CAREER PLANNING

The remainder of this text is based on a comprehensive model of career development which is broken into a series of steps. It incorporates many different aspects of the theories described previously, particularly from the trait-and-factor and developmental categories. The paradigm is composed of the following stages:

- *Self-assessment:* During this stage you begin the process of career planning by gaining awareness about yourself to help answer the question "who am I" as it relates to academics and careers. This step includes evaluating your values, skills, interests, and personality. (These four items will collectively be referred to as your *Personal Career Profile* throughout this textbook.) It can also include other aspects of self such as beliefs, talents, gifts, passions, needs, and lifestyle preferences, but in this book we will focus on the four components mentioned above. This self-knowledge can be evaluated by reflecting on how your past experiences and information you have collected through career assessments have helped you understand who you are today. This is a critical step because it grounds the career exploration process and provides direction throughout.

- *Research:* Equipped with self-information, you can then begin to research and explore both major and career options which will allow you to express yourself in the work world through your values, skills, interests, and personality. You can do research through books, online resources, and by gathering information from people in your given field(s) of interest.

- *Try it out:* After gathering information about yourself and your educational and vocational options, you must assess the fit between who you are (your Personal Career Profile), and your options. While reading about majors and careers is useful, it is far more powerful to actually experience them. Trying out majors may involve taking courses and interviewing students and professors. You can gain this exposure to careers by job shadowing, taking a part-time job, volunteering, getting involved in student organizations, or through acquiring an internship. It is crucial to reflect back on your self-information and evaluate the match you may or may not feel between yourself and this major or career.

- *Job/Internship search:* Once you have gathered self, major, and career information and tried out one or multiple majors or career paths, you are ready to begin the process of finding and securing an internship or full-time position. This step requires you to learn how to effectively market your skills and experiences through your resumes, cover letters, and interviews. This step will not be covered extensively in this textbook; however, please see *Ready or Not: The Art and Science of the Job Search* for a detailed guide to the job search process.

THE CAREER DEVELOPMENT PROCESS

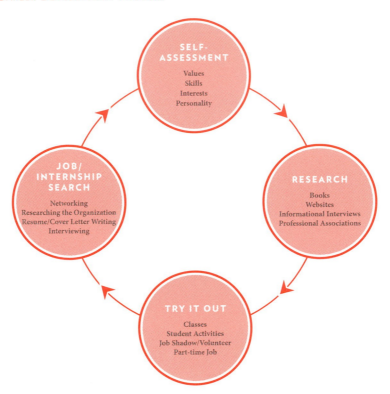

The career development process is lifelong and will require you to make many career decisions along the way. According to the Bureau of Labor Statistics, the average person will have four careers and thirteen jobs over their lifespan. Because of this phenomenon, you will most likely cycle through the four steps described above multiple times and often in a nonlinear way. For example, you might be trying to confirm your interest (self-assessment) in marketing by taking an internship (trying out the career). However, you then might realize that marketing is not the best fit for you, consider other career options (research), go back and reflect on your other interests (self-assessment), apply for more internships (job search), and explore a different potential career in human resources (trying out the career).

Each time you cycle through the process, you gain more information about yourself, more clarity about your values, interests, and personality, and more skills to apply to the next job or career. This book will systematically take you through the process of exploring who you are, uncover resources and methods to explore majors and careers, and finally, provide strategies for making decisions, setting goals, and gaining experience to make you marketable in your future career. We hope that, equipped with these tools, you will begin your career journey with informed confidence.

SETTING THE STAGE

"We have, all of us, an impulse toward actualizing more of our potentialities, toward self-actualization... [This is also an impulse] to be the best, the very best you are capable of becoming. If you deliberately plan to be less than you are capable of being, then I warn you that you'll be deeply unhappy for the rest of your life."

ABRAHAM MASLOW, PSYCHOLOGIST

INTRODUCTION

Before launching into the career planning process described previously, it is important for you to understand key foundational concepts that set the stage for your personal and career development. Gaining awareness of what motivates you, and of the beliefs that underpin your attitude toward career development in general, will help you to make more conscious decisions. This increased clarity will improve your chances for success and contentment, both now and on your future career path. As Maslow implies in the quote above, the choice to realize your full potential is entirely your own.

MOTIVATION TO WORK

As the world of work has evolved, various psychological models have been created to explain the needs that are met through work, and the corresponding motivations that drive people to do their work. Abraham Maslow was a psychologist who developed a hierarchy of needs, which provides a framework for exploring the relationship between motivation and career development.

Learning Objectives

» Understand what motivates your self-exploration and development

» Appreciate the power of beliefs in the career planning process

» Identify beliefs related to choosing a major or career

Deficiency Needs

Everyone enters the world aware of their most basic needs for food and shelter; you also need to be protected and to find safety. Once you feel protected through relationships, security, food, and shelter, the need for self-esteem arises and is met through significant accomplishments and achieved prestige or status. Maslow's Hierarchy visually represents the relationship between these needs; the lowest rung in the hierarchy demonstrates the most essential human needs, which must be gratified before moving to the next level. Collectively, the bottom four needs on the hierarchy are termed *deficiency needs* because each need must be satisfied before subsequent needs surface.

Growth Needs

Once the deficiency needs are satisfied, higher needs emerge, constituting the remaining four levels on the hierarchy, which are known as *growth needs*. Fulfilling your growth needs begins as you strive for mental growth through knowledge, and for external growth through the need for aesthetic beauty in your environment. At the higher stages, you are capable of self-actualization, meaning that you become more certain of what you were uniquely designed to do, and you feel able to reach your full potential. And finally, at the top of these eight levels is transcendence, in which you are able to rise above your unconscious patterns of behavior and become freer to be your truest self.

8-LEVEL
HIERARCHY OF NEEDS

Transcendence
Helping others to
self-actualize

Self-Actualization
Personal growth, self-fulfillment

Aesthetic Needs
Beauty, balance, form, etc.

Cognitive Needs
Knowledge, meaning, self-awareness

Esteem Needs
Achievement, status, responsibility, reputation

Belongingness & Love Needs
Family, affection, relationships, work groups, etc.

Safety Needs
Protection, security, order, law, limits, stability, etc.

Biological & Physiological Needs
Basic life needs – air, food, drink, shelter, warmth, sex, sleep, etc.

© *The Hierarchy of Needs concept was devised by Abraham Maslow (1954).*

Needs and Career Planning

Maslow's Hierarchy of Needs helps provide insight into why you will prioritize your deficiency needs (as you must have food, shelter, safety, relationships, and self-esteem) when you are engaging in the career planning process and making decisions. For example, if you are born into a low-income family, the main motivation to work likely will be to provide food, clothing, and a place to live. If you live in a high-crime or violent neighborhood, you might then be motivated to find work that would allow you to afford housing in a safer area. If this need is met, then you may begin thinking about a career path that offers you the kind of personal and professional relationships you desire. Perhaps you begin to seek a boss who challenges you, or colleagues who collaborate on projects. Once your basic needs are met, and you are surrounded by a supportive environment, you may begin to focus more intently on accomplishing goals that provide you with more responsibility, status, and opportunities to achieve.

Additionally, life circumstances will impact what level you focus on. For instance during a recession, you could lose your job, and suddenly your priorities shift. You may have had the luxury of being selective about the work environment and level of responsibility you were given in your previous position; however now, with no job, it is likely that once again the need for food and shelter drives your motivation to find and keep work. Once your deficiency needs are met, you can begin to consider cognitive, aesthetic, self-actualization, and transcendence needs. But these growth needs are not essential to living, so what is it that will motivate you to achieve these needs?

SELF-AUTHORSHIP AS A PATH TO HIGHER GROWTH

Very often what motivates continued growth and development is pain or discomfort. When you become unhappy and discontented enough to be willing to look at what is really happening in your life, you open the door to change. These uncomfortable life circumstances and events may cause you to question who you really are. Your identity may be shaken to the very core; therefore, you will likely find yourself wanting to step back and reflect on your responses to life thus far.

Recall that the suggested first step of beginning the career journey is exploring your identity. Marcia Baxter-Magolda, a student development theorist, offers a pathway to discover yourself, which involves three distinct phases of identity development: (1) being externally defined, (2) entering/being at a crossroads, and (3) becoming internally defined.

Phase One

In phase one (externally defined), you will likely be largely influenced by your parents, educational settings, and media as you make decisions, including your consideration of majors and careers. You may not even be aware of the fact that your identity has been highly influenced by who others think you are or should be. For example, you may believe that you should pursue a degree in economics because that is what your dad and siblings did. It is common for students to enter college in this stage.

Phase Two

In phase two (crossroads), you begin to question the ideas you have about who you are and what you want to do with your life. You may begin to deeply ponder where you got those ideas and whether or not they make sense for you. It could be that through experiencing coursework, a volunteer position, a part-time job, or an internship in a particular area, you start to recognize that something is not working for you. For instance, you began taking courses in economics and learned more about potential future careers, and later realized that you were not as excited about those opportunities as you thought you would be. Perhaps economics isn't working for you because you realized you were seeking to meet others' expectations rather than your own needs or desires.

Often people encounter these crossroads experiences during college and into the beginning of their professional careers. It is at these crossroads that you may choose to pursue Maslow's growth needs (discussed in the previous section), recognizing that though your basic needs have been met, there is an internal discomfort that is getting your attention and motivating you to explore and potentially make different choices.

Phase Three

In phase three (internally defined), you recognize that there is often a disconnect between following the path others have set out for you versus coming to understand and embrace yourself as a unique, independent individual. You gain clarity on your core personal values, which provide direction as you navigate through life. You begin to hear and trust your internal voice, developing the ability to respect, appreciate, and consider the opinions of others, while simultaneously evaluating your own needs and wants as you make decisions. Returning to our economics example, after experiencing the divide between your interests and pursuing the "family path," you realize that you appreciate the strong economics and business heritage you have been given, but decide to pursue a completely different academic and career path in education.

Shifting through these phases will lead you toward self-authorship. The progression outlined in the Journey Toward Self-Authorship chart may help raise your awareness about knowing who you are and how you've come to be where you are in the world. By taking these steps, you will likely grow personally and professionally. You will be one step closer to reaching your highest potential, one step closer to what Maslow termed self-actualization. This awareness empowers you to make choices that will enhance your college experience, allowing this time to possibly be a significant "crossroads" in your journey. See ACTIVITIES 1.1 and 1.2 at the end of the chapter for an opportunity to begin reflecting on what is motivating you to work and study, as well as where you are on your own path toward self-authorship. As we delve into the more concrete elements of career planning throughout this text, you will be asked to reflect back on self-authorship, allowing you to integrate what you are learning into the context of this larger developmental process.

JOURNEY TOWARD SELF-AUTHORSHIP

Phases	Phase One: Externally Defined	Phase Two: Crossroads	Phase Three: Internally Defined
Key Characteristics	Believes authority	Questions plan	Chooses own beliefs
	Defined by others	Dilemma of external definition	Chooses own identity
	Requires approval of others		

This table was adapted from Baxter-Magolda's Theory of Self-Authorship.

WHERE IS MY VOICE?

Maureen was a freshman trying to figure out what she wanted to do with her life. Before coming to college, she decided that she was going to major in religious studies. She figured this must be the best major for her because she found it to be somewhat interesting and her plan was to become a professor one day. As part of her exploration process she decided to talk to a religious studies professor (Dr. Heyne) to find out more about what it was like to get a Ph.D. and to work in this field.

Dr. Heyne described the steps to earning a Ph.D., which include intensive course work, qualifying exams, research, writing and defending one's dissertation. He also

(continued)

explained that the average graduate student completed the degree in four to seven years. Maureen's eyes widened and she began to feel overwhelmed as she imagined herself undertaking this enormous task. She began to realize how much time she would need to spend alone reading, researching, and writing. How would she get through all of that? "Won't I be lonely and exhausted?" she wondered. She also considered the time commitment; how would that affect her desire to begin a family?

As she continued talking with Dr. Heyne she also learned about the continued pressures on professors to research, gain tenure, serve on committees, teach, and mentor. Again, she became concerned about her other priorities such as her need for interaction with others and her quality time with family and friends. She also started to think about how much she wanted to see tangible results of her work, and how she enjoyed persuading others through brainstorming and implementing her creative ideas.

After concluding her interview with Dr. Heyne, Maureen began to reflect on her path. She began to realize that many things she had learned about didn't seem to align with what she truly wanted. Why did she feel so compelled to get a Ph.D. and become a faculty member? What made her feel like this was her only option? As she pondered these questions, she realized that there were multiple factors at play. Both of her parents were encouraging her to pursue the academic world because they were providing her an opportunity to gain an advanced degree, an option they never had. She also realized that our culture values higher education and that she could earn a level of prestige and admiration in pursuing this path. Additionally, her instructors were encouraging her to strongly consider a career as a professor because she excelled in the coursework and seemed consistently engaged. Perplexed and confused, she asked, "But where am I in all of this? What do I truly want?"

Maureen decided to delve into her career planning further. She wanted to determine her life and her career path, and realized she was pursuing a dream that was not her own. She deeply desired to learn more about herself, who she really was, what she truly loved, what felt like a good fit for her, and what would be meaningful. With renewed energy, she committed to the challenging process of navigating the unknown. Though she felt fear, she also experienced a calm certainty and happiness in knowing that she was going to be true to *herself* above all.

It is important to realize that meeting your higher level needs and reaching internal self-definition is undoubtedly a lifelong process that will be influenced by every decision and action taken along the way. As you gain experiences and reflect, you will enhance self-understanding, gain increased clarity, and will know more quickly and easily how to make choices that are truly satisfying.

BELIEFS

As we launch into the more concrete phases of career development including self, major, and career exploration, pause to inventory your current attitude. What thoughts and feelings arise as you think about figuring out your next steps? Investigating the beliefs that underlie your current mindset will open the door for further consciousness, and give you the opportunity to make more deliberate choices.

Have you ever noticed that certain thoughts keep popping up in your head, over and over? It might be a positive thought, like "I am an awesome basketball player." You get energized by that thought, and every time you're on the court, you are confident and self-assured. Other thoughts may be negative, such as "I'm not a good test taker." And every time you sit down to take one, you feel nervous and unsure of yourself.

Whether positive or negative, our thoughts about ourselves or our worldview are the ones that get most charged with emotional energy, because they are part of our identity ("I am …"), or the way we uniquely view the world ("People are…"). We call these charged-up thoughts *beliefs,* which are simply thoughts we invest with energy and uncritically believe to be true. Beliefs tend to perpetuate themselves, even if experience suggests they may not be true. For example, we might get A's and B's on several tests in a row, but still believe it was a fluke, because after all, "I'm not a good test-taker." Beliefs color the way we view ourselves.

The Origin of Beliefs

Where do beliefs come from? Often they spring from the meaning that we grant an event or situation. If you had a bad experience in your first semester of high school algebra, you may interpret this as meaning that no matter how hard you try, you are never going to "get" algebra. Once we decide the meaning of something, we are often resistant to changing that interpretation, no matter how irrational it may be.

Family members, teachers, and friends also influence our beliefs, and the more externally defined we are, the stronger we will feel their influence. If these people are positive and affirming of our abilities and character, we will likely believe the same things about ourselves. Unfortunately, the reverse is also true—if they disapprove of or belittle us, we may take on disempowering beliefs. The media also influences our beliefs about who we are and what the world is. Whether real or fictional, compelling stories about über-successful people or beautiful models that would make anyone feel less worthy by comparison may fuel our self-doubt and diminish our self-esteem.

Ultimately, though, more than events, people, or media, the core beliefs we already have about ourselves, called *schemata* (see box), are the magnets that allow other beliefs to stick to us, or not.

SCHEMATA—OUR CORE BELIEFS

As powerful a hold as they seem to have over us, the funny thing is that beliefs—positive or negative—are simply thoughts that we're empowering with mental and emotional energy. Even stranger, we often hold on to negatively charged beliefs even though they do not serve us. Why? Because they've become part of our identity—of who we think we are.

Most of us have one or two deeply held beliefs about ourselves or the world, which psychologists call schemata. These often simple beliefs were formed when our mind tried to make sense of our experience. When negatively charged, we may not even be conscious of our schemata, but that doesn't prevent them from causing us psychological pain and limitation. Ironically, they may be so central to our self-concept that we hold onto them for dear life:

- I'm an unworthy person.
- I don't have what it takes.
- The world is a dangerous place.
- I will never fit in.

If you think such a core belief is holding you back in your career development, or in life in general, working with a professional counselor or therapist who specializes in cognitive-behavioral techniques may be life-changing. Contact your school's counseling center for information.

The Power of Beliefs

You can probably tell that, in general, positively charged beliefs are more constructive than their opposite. These beliefs contribute to our self-esteem, making it easier for us to learn and to achieve our goals. Negatively charged beliefs can obstruct our learning and progress, making it much more challenging to succeed at anything we do. Whether positively or negatively charged, our beliefs constantly (and often insidiously) affect our lives.

For nine years—an unusually long time—the world record for running the mile held steady at just above four minutes. This led some people to believe that the four-minute mile was a barrier that would never be broken. In 1954, British athlete Roger Bannister ran a mile in 3:59. It is said that in the following year, 37 runners broke four minutes, and 300 more did so the next year. Track experts never actually believed that four minutes was a physical barrier, but this story nevertheless illustrates the power of belief—once it was shown to be possible, others believed they could do it too, and they did. This is an example of a "self-fulfilling prophecy"—believe it's possible, and it's much more likely to happen.

A self-fulfilling prophecy may also lead to unwanted results, which could be considered self-sabotage. What if Roger Bannister had believed that the four-minute mile really was a barrier? What happens to a student who believes she will never be a good test-taker, so she stops studying for tests altogether?

When it comes to forging a path through college by choosing an interesting major and starting to consider post-college career options, positive beliefs will help you tremendously, and negative or disempowering beliefs may block your progress altogether, as they blocked people who believed the four-minute mile was a real barrier. It's vitally important to get clear about your beliefs so that, as Abraham Maslow advocated, you can actualize your deepest potentials and realize your fondest dreams. See ACTIVITY 1.3 at the end of the chapter to explore your beliefs about your abilities.

Changing Your Beliefs

Fortunately, there are ways to become aware of our beliefs. Awareness is always the first step toward change. After all, if you aren't first aware of a problem you won't be able to take the necessary steps to change or fix it.

To become aware of your beliefs, take some time to become intentionally aware of your "self-talk"—the mostly involuntary thoughts that are constantly present in your mind. Paying attention to your thoughts may seem difficult at first, but the more you do it, the easier it becomes.

Do you believe in your ability to find a major and career that you will like? Do you believe that you will be able to succeed in it? Examples of self-affirming beliefs may include:

- I'll definitely find an interesting major.
- There is an exciting career waiting out there for me.
- I will be successful in college.
- I will start where I am, and get there one step at a time.
- I deserve to have satisfying work.
- I have the tools to make good decisions.
- My motivation and efforts will determine my success.
- I'm a worthy person, no matter what major or career I choose.

It's also important to check inside and see if you hold any beliefs that could undermine your quest for an engaging major or career. Examples of such beliefs may include:

- I won't be able to find an interesting major.
- I'll probably end up in a job I hate.
- I doubt I'll be successful in college—I don't have what it takes.
- I don't know where to start.
- It will be really hard to find enjoyable work.
- I don't know how to make decisions.
- There's no reason to try, because I probably won't succeed.
- My self-worth is dependent on choosing the right major or career.

See ACTIVITY 1.4 at the end of the chapter to explore your beliefs about finding the right major or career, and about your general career development.

If you're unclear as to what your negatively charged beliefs are, reflect on your fears. Typically, every fear has one or more beliefs that underlie it. For example, underneath the fear of making the wrong choice about your major might be the belief, "If I choose the wrong major, I'll be stuck with it until I graduate." See ACTIVITY 1.5 to explore the beliefs under your fears.

Once you gain clarity about your beliefs, you can work to intentionally cultivate the positive ones:

- Affirm a positive belief consciously by saying it silently or out loud to yourself, on a regular basis. Write your belief on a piece of paper and tape it to your mirror as a reminder, or create a screensaver for your computer that displays your positive beliefs.

- Associate positive beliefs with positive images and feelings. If you believe "I will find an interesting major," spend a few minutes each day imagining yourself in interesting classes, and allow yourself to feel the positive emotions associated with that experience.

While you're cultivating the positive, you can also work to release negative or limiting beliefs:

- Consider the origin of each negative belief. Is it really yours, or did you learn it from your parents, friends, or the media? If so, do you need to keep believing it? (For example, if you realize that part of you believes that "There's no way I'll find a good major," ask yourself the source. Do you have a friend who is so negative about the possibility of success in college that you started to be negative too?)

- Ask yourself, do I really believe this is true, or is thinking this just a bad habit?

- Question the belief's validity. Ask yourself, is this really true? Can I really know it, for a fact? (Using the previous example, you might ask, "Can I really know it's true that I won't find a major that is a good fit for me? Can I predict the future, after all? How could I really know, anyway?")

- Ask yourself, what does this belief do for me? What do I get by believing this? (For example, you might discover that you hold onto that same belief because you're afraid you might appear arrogant or too optimistic if you believed otherwise.)

CONCLUSION

Knowing that your needs motivate you helps answer the daunting question of what will propel you forward and help you stay committed to the path of self and career exploration. Part of that journey is becoming aware of how others have impacted your view of who you are and the beliefs you have developed. As you begin your career development journey, reflect on your career aspirations and dreams freely. Consider the knowledge you will gain about yourself, academic disciplines, and the world of work. Set your intentions and trust that through honoring your passions and fully engaging in the career exploration process, your path will become open and clear. Remember you are not making a lifelong commitment; you are choosing the next best step in your academic and career path.

CHAPTER 1

ACTIVITIES

ACTIVITY 1.1   **IDENTIFY YOUR MOTIVATION TO STUDY AND WORK**

Go back and review Maslow's Hierarchy of Needs. As you reflect on his theory of human motivation, ask yourself what is motivating you to pursue your studies and your career. Is it the basic human needs? Safety needs? Love and belonging? Self-esteem? Self-actualization? Perhaps you are being motivated by more than one need simultaneously. Once you have pinpointed the needs that resonate with where you are right now, write about how being motivated by that need affects the career options you are considering. For example, if you are most worried about meeting your biological needs you may be pursuing a high-paying career path.

ACTIVITY 1.2   **REFLECT ON INFLUENCES**

Take a moment to consider all the external influences (parents, family, friends, teachers, school, where you grew up, media, technology, celebrities, heroes) in your life thus far and write them down.

- What impact does each of these influences have in your life (the way you define yourself and the decisions you make)?

- How do you feel about each of these outside factors and the influence each has had on your life?

- What were your first visions of a career you wanted to pursue? Who or what impacted those initial visions?

- Describe two important life-learning experiences (positive or negative) and describe how they have influenced your career interests.

ACTIVITY 1.3   **I THINK I CAN / CAN'T**

As Henry Ford famously put it, "Whether you think you can or can't, you're right." What beliefs do you have about your abilities? Write out five sentences beginning with "I can" and then write out five sentences beginning with "I can't."

Choose one positive "I can" belief to affirm, and one negative "I can't" belief to release, using the techniques described in this chapter.

ACTIVITY 1.4   **DISCOVER YOUR BELIEFS ABOUT FINDING THE RIGHT MAJOR OR CAREER**

This activity will help you become aware of beliefs you have about finding the right major or career. Write down as many beliefs as you can, positive and/or negative, by responding to the following:

- What do I believe about finding the right major or career?
- What do I believe about my abilities to find the right major or career?
- If you're having trouble articulating your beliefs, think about your recent actions in this area (or lack thereof). What beliefs might underlie your actions or inaction?

You can also try finishing sentences that begin with these words and phrases:

- "I believe that finding an interesting major…"
- "I believe that finding an interesting career …"

Think each phrase silently and wait, allowing your beliefs to present themselves when they're ready.

ACTIVITY 1.5   **DISCOVER THE BELIEFS UNDER YOUR FEARS**

Write down three of your biggest fears about finding a major, succeeding in college, or finding a job you like. Then, write down the belief underlying that fear, and the source of that belief.

Fear: Underlying Beliefs (Source)
Example:
I'll end up in a job I hate: It's impossible to find fulfilling work. (Neither Mom nor Dad ever had jobs they liked.)

ACTIVITY 1.6   **DISCOVER BELIEFS ABOUT YOUR GOALS**

Write down a specific goal that you currently have (e.g. "Interview a professional news editor to help me decide whether I want to major in journalism."). Next, write down positive and negative beliefs that you have about achieving this specific goal:

- Positive beliefs (*example:* "I'll easily find a news editor who wants to tell me about their work.")
- Negative or limiting beliefs (*example:* "What news editor is going to want to talk to me?")

CHAPTER 1

SUMMARY & KEY POINTS

- As you plan for your future, it is valuable to reflect on the psychological factors at play in motivating your actions. By gaining an understanding of the levels of human development, you have the opportunity to fulfill your highest potential.

- A critical step in your career journey is challenging yourself to think about what has influenced who you are and where you want to go. College is an opportune time to explore these questions, empowering you to become the author of your own life.

- Because beliefs—positive or negative—are often "self-fulfilling prophecies," it is worthwhile to intentionally cultivate positive beliefs, and release negative ones.

VALUES

*"When everything else about a job is stripped away, the values remain.
'Why do this job? Why work in the first place?'"*

HOWARD FIGLER, CAREER COUNSELOR & AUTHOR

INTRODUCTION

In this chapter you'll build the first of the four components of
your Personal Career Profile (values, skills, interests, and personality) by assessing your values. As the above quotation suggests,
your values will greatly influence your career choices. Values are
those things that are important to you, and they affect how you
think, what you feel, and what decisions you make. You may
not always be aware of your values, yet conscious or not, they
steer your every action. By exploring and better understanding
this important aspect of self, you will be able to make more
conscious decisions that will improve your chances for success
and satisfaction in college, and later, in your chosen occupation.

Learning Objectives

» Understand the importance of
knowing your values in order
to make the best possible career
decisions

» Explore the origin of your
values, and learn what to do
when values conflict

» Assess your values in order to
gain insight into the types of
work that will most satisfy you

DIFFERENT ROLES, DIFFERENT VALUES

We each have values for different roles in our life. Here are some
examples of work values:

- Having a flexible schedule

- Doing work that helps others

- Having a lot of vacation time

Here are some examples of academic values:

- Getting good grades
- Taking classes that interest me
- Keeping a balanced academic workload

Because we tend to be satisfied when we're acting in harmony with our values, knowing what they are is essential for opening the door to a fulfilling major or career. On the other hand, if we're not clear about what's important to us, we may end up in a school or work situation that is so unsatisfying that we can hardly bear to get out of bed each morning. In fact, people often leave a job or career only because it doesn't satisfy one of their values. Knowing your values will help you make better decisions, so that you're more likely to end up where you want to be—instead of somewhere else. To take your first steps toward identifying your values, see ACTIVITIES 2.1 and 2.2.

VALUES—SUBJECTIVE AND PERSONAL

Our values are influenced by our family, friends, religious and cultural background, the media, and our past experiences. You may have strongly-held values based on those influences, but others may not be so strong. For example, maybe your dad is a corporate executive and has always harped on the importance of getting an MBA in order to ensure a high income, and you came to college without ever doubting that this would be your path. But after taking some classes and reflecting, you realize that it's more important to you to do humanitarian work that may not bring in as much money as your dad's line of work. You realize—in a shift from Baxter-Magolda's external to a more internal self-definition—that "making good money," while it would be nice, is really your dad's value, not yours.

Values are largely subjective; for example, they may be influenced by the historical period in which we live. Your grandparents or great-grandparents likely placed a high value on frugality because of their experiences during the Great Depression. On the other hand, you may not place so high a value on thrift. Or you may believe, like your parents, that working hard makes you a better person, but are surprised to make a friend who values their leisure time and believes just as strongly that time outside of work makes him a better person.

People may define a given value in different ways. Take "success." Many people want to achieve success, but what does "success" really mean? One person might define it as making a six-figure salary. Another might say, as did magazine founder B.C. Forbes, that someone who "has done his level best … is a success, even though the world may write him down as a failure." Or like anthropologist Margaret Mead, we might define success as "the contributions an individual makes to her or his fellow human beings." As you reflect on each of your values, especially abstractions such as "success," "meaningful work," or "happiness," consider what they uniquely mean to you. To take your exploration of values even deeper, see ACTIVITY 2.3.

CONFLICTING VALUES, CHANGING VALUES

Another important reason to be aware of your values is because they may sometimes conflict, which can impede your ability to make a decision. When this happens, it will be helpful to consider which of your values are in conflict, and then to figure out which one is the *most* important to your career planning.

JEREMY'S VALUES CLASH—WHAT WOULD YOU DO?

When Jeremy was a sophomore in college, he found a part-time job at a popular restaurant near campus. Jeremy liked to keep busy, and also liked having extra spending money. His job as a server turned out to be a smooth ride, and he was able to fit it in between a busy social life and demanding class schedule.

Soon after he began his junior year, Jeremy's boss requested that he work an extra Saturday night shift on Homecoming weekend, when thousands of alumni would flood the town and keep the restaurant busy until the late hours. Jeremy agreed. As the week approached, though, Jeremy learned that his best friend Daniel's 21st birthday party was set for the same Saturday night. If he worked the extra shift, he would miss the party.

Jeremy was at a loss. He valued his job and respected his boss, who had never before requested that he work an additional shift. The restaurant was already understaffed, and it was unlikely that extra help could be found at the last minute. On the other hand, Daniel's 21st birthday party was sure to be a blast, and it would never come again. Daniel also might be disappointed if Jeremy didn't show.

Two of Jeremy's values—loyalty to his job, and loyalty to his best friend—were in

(continued)

JEREMY'S VALUES CLASH *(continued)*

conflict. Though it might seem that whatever choice he made, Jeremy would end up the loser, there is a bright side: Jeremy is becoming conscious of his values and the complexities involved in decision making. By confronting this situation with awareness, Jeremy is bound to improve his decision-making capabilities, as well as increase the odds that he will discover work that satisfies his core values.

If you were in Jeremy's shoes, what would you do?

Values conflicts may happen when you're considering potential careers. Maybe you've discovered a career that pays well (a value of high importance for you), but after more research you discover that it may not provide enough job security (another value of high importance for you). In order to decide whether to pursue this career, you will need to prioritize your values and consider all the options.

Our values are also influenced by where we are in Maslow's Hierarchy of Needs (see CHAPTER 1). If we are focused on fulfilling Love/Belonging Needs, we tend to value activities associated with that level—for example, finding a boyfriend or girlfriend. Once we have fulfilled those needs, our values may shift to the next level; for example, you might focus next on improving your self-esteem by doing well at your job and getting a promotion. To assess your specific work values, see ACTIVITY 2.4.

CONCLUSION

Becoming aware of your values is essential to the process of choosing a satisfying major and aiming toward a fulfilling career. By knowing what is most important to you, you are likely to make better decisions about these serious matters.

In the next chapter, you will explore your skills as you continue putting together these separate puzzle pieces of self into a more complete picture of your life and future work.

CHAPTER 2

ACTIVITIES

ACTIVITY 2.1 **IMAGINE THE WORST JOB EVER**

Write about the worst job you could possibly imagine. Answer as many of the following as possible: What do you do? What are the working conditions? What are the pay and benefits? Whom do you work with? Whom do you serve? What services do you provide or products do you make? What type of supervisor do you have? What are the requirements and demands of the job?

When you're finished, reread what you wrote and pick out the values that you see. What did you learn about yourself?

ACTIVITY 2.2 **ENVISION YOUR DREAM JOB**

Write about your dream job. Imagine it in as much detail as possible, using as many of your five senses as possible to describe it. What would the perfect job look like for you?

When you're finished, reread what you wrote and pick out the values that you see. What did you learn about yourself?

ACTIVITY 2.3 **WRITE YOUR EULOGY**

Imagine that it's many years from now. You've lived a satisfying life that was full and complete. How were your most deeply-held values reflected in the work you did? What and how did you give back to the world? If someone were to give a eulogy about your working life, what would they say?

ACTIVITY 2.4   **ASSESS YOUR WORK VALUES**

Mark each of the 35 work values below as L, M, or H (L=low or no importance to me, M=medium importance to me, H=high importance to me).

_____ **Advancement**: there are ample promotional opportunities in my organization or career field

_____ **Benefits**: my job offers benefits such as vacation and sick leave, health and life insurance plans, and retirement plans

_____ **Challenge**: my work challenges me

_____ **Colleagues**: my supervisor and coworkers are supportive and friendly

_____ **Competition**: my workplace is a competitive environment

_____ **Creativity**: I have opportunities to express my creativity

_____ **Ethics**: I respect my employer and do not experience situations that could conflict with my ethical standards

_____ **Flexibility (scheduling hours)**: I have flexibility in setting my schedule of work hours

_____ **Flexibility (while working)**: I have flexibility in planning my time while at work

_____ **Goals and Results**: my work is goal-oriented and I see the results of my efforts

_____ **Independence**: I have autonomy in my work tasks and am minimally supervised

_____ **Interest**: my work is interesting to me and a very important part of my life

_____ **Leadership**: my work offers leadership opportunities

_____ **Learning (High)**: my work requires ongoing learning

_____ **Learning (Low)**: after initial training, my work requires little learning

_____ **Location**: my workplace is close to my home and commuting time is minimal

_____ **Management**: my work provides opportunities to supervise and manage others

_____ **Moral Fulfillment**: my work contributes to my higher ideals

_____ **Pay and Profit**: I am well compensated for my work

_____ **People**: my work involves significant people contact

_____ **Power**: I have power and authority to make decisions and set policy

_____ **Pressure and Pace (High)**: the pressure and pace of my work are high

_____ **Pressure and Pace (Low)**: the pressure and pace of my work are low

_____ **Prestige**: my title and/or work is prestigious and commands respect and attention

_____ **Recognition**: I receive positive feedback for a job well done

_____ **Security**: my job security is high

_____ **Supervision**: I receive high quality supervision

_____ **Teamwork (High)**: much of my work is done on teams

_____ **Teamwork (Low)**: my job requires little, if any, teamwork

_____ **Training**: the training program is excellent and thorough

_____ **Travel (High)**: I travel extensively

_____ **Travel (Low)**: I rarely travel or do not travel

_____ **Variety**: my work offers variety in tasks

_____ **Workspace**: I have a private workspace or office

_____ **Work/Life Balance**: I feel comfortable with the balance between my work life and personal and/or family life

Next, create a list of your top work values by writing down all the values you marked H. If you've thought of values that aren't on the above list, feel free to add them to the list.

Once you've written this list, rank them in order. What are your top five values?

Obviously, the above list is not exhaustive. Continue exploring your values by reflecting on both work and non-work experiences you have during and after college.

CHAPTER 2

SUMMARY & KEY POINTS

- Knowing your values will help you make better decisions.
- Our values are influenced by the people we know and our society.
- We tend to be most satisfied when our work corresponds to our values.

SKILLS

"Happiness comes when we test our skills towards some meaningful purpose."

JOHN STOSSEL, JOURNALIST

INTRODUCTION

In this chapter you will build the next component of your Personal Career Profile by examining your skills. A skill is the ability, from training or experience, to do something well. Knowledge of what skills are required in an occupation that interests you is vital, and will help you select skills you need to improve to enter and succeed in that field. It's also important to know the skills you enjoy using the most, because you'll be employing your skills all day long in any occupation you choose. As the above quotation suggests, if you put your skills to use in a purposeful way, you will increase the potential that your work will satisfy you.

TYPES OF SKILLS

The word "skill" is based on a word from Middle English which meant "to distinguish." When you're ready to look for work, your skills are among the most important attributes that will help *distinguish* you from other applicants. But this original sense of the word is also a reminder of an important fact: skills also help you to stand out and excel on the job.

There are three categories of skills. The first category is *transferable skills* (see next page), sometimes called "soft skills." Because

Learning Objectives

» Appreciate the importance of knowing your skills in order to further your career development

» Understand the three categories of skills—transferable skills, specialized knowledge, and personal attributes

» Identify your current skills, skills you enjoy using, and skills you need to improve

most work environments need people with these skills, they are the ones you will "transfer," or take with you, wherever you go. Communication skills such as writing or presenting, leadership skills such as coordinating or delegating, and teamwork skills such as collaborating or compromising, are all examples of transferable skills. In college you will have many opportunities to enhance the transferable skills you already have, and to develop new ones. You may then transfer these skills to an internship or volunteer experience, and later, to a paying job.

TOP SKILLS AND PERSONAL ATTRIBUTES

In recent years, the National Association of Colleges and Employers reported that the people most sought after by employers have had transferable skills and personal attributes such as:

- Communication skills
- Teamwork skills (works well with others)
- Motivation/Initiative
- Interpersonal skills (relates well to others)
- Strong work ethic
- Analytical skills
- Flexibility/Adaptability
- Computer skills
- Detail-oriented
- Organizational skills

The breadth of knowledge you acquire as a college student means that you are particularly likely to develop many of the above skills and attributes both inside and outside the classroom (at least if you take advantage of the many opportunities to get involved both on and off campus). (See CHAPTER 11 for ways to get involved.)

The second category is *specialized knowledge*, sometimes called "hard skills." Specialized knowledge is likely to be relevant to one specific job or career, but not to others. For example, in the field of construction, knowing how to operate a bulldozer is specialized knowledge. In the field of computer programming, knowing how to write a software application using Java is specialized knowledge. But if a computer programmer decides to become a construction worker, her boss isn't likely to care that she's a wiz at Java. Most occupations require some specialized knowledge. Sometimes you may receive on-the-job training to acquire necessary specialized knowledge, but for certain fields (such as nursing or accounting), you may need to already have the knowledge (and possibly a license as well) before applying.

The third and last category of skills consists of *personal attributes* such as initiative, flexibility, and punctuality. Some personal attributes may be closely tied to aspects of your personality. Others may be influenced by factors such as genetics or your upbringing. You may find it easy to improve upon certain characteristics, while others may take significant time and effort to cultivate. But with motivation and persistence, like Ben Franklin (see box), you may be able to develop or improve many of these attributes. In CHAPTER 5, you will learn much more about personality preferences and how those might enhance or inhibit your personal attributes and other skills.

BENJAMIN FRANKLIN, SELF-IMPROVEMENT EXPERT

Founding Father Benjamin Franklin took seriously the task of improving himself by intentionally working to develop certain personal attributes. At the age of 20, Franklin developed a list of attributes that he wished to improve, including frugality, honesty, and work ethic. He focused on a single attribute for one week at a time, keeping written track of his progress. At the end of the week, he would evaluate himself and choose a new attribute to practice for the following week. He continued this self-improvement endeavor in various ways throughout his life. It's probably no accident that Franklin became one of the most successful men in America, and was able to retire from his work as a printer at the age of 42 in order to pursue many other fascinating careers, including political theorist, inventor, politician, statesman, and diplomat.

HOW TO IDENTIFY YOUR SKILLS

Think about what you've accomplished so far in your life, as well as the paid and un-paid work that you've had. In order to identify the skills you've used, you might take one accomplishment or job and break it down into the various tasks that it required, and then break each of those tasks into the specific transferable skills, specialized knowledge, and personal attributes that were necessary to successfully execute it. For example, say last summer you worked as a camp counselor. One major task included managing the junior counselors. The *transferable skills* involved in this task included *planning* and *scheduling* their workday, *mentoring* them, *leading* them, and *communicating* with them and the professional staff. *Specialized knowledge* for this task was proficiency with the camp's scheduling software. Personal attributes you demonstrated for this task included having a *positive attitude*, being *detail-oriented*, and *being supportive*. If you need help identifying your skills, visit an advisor at your campus career center, and see ACTIVITIES 3.1 and 3.2.

DEVELOPING SKILLS

As mentioned previously, knowing the skills that are necessary to enter a specific occupation or career field is essential. Fortunately—as shown in Danny's Story below—transferable skills and specialized knowledge can be intentionally developed based on what you need or want to do. Danny's Story also illustrates that while it's important to choose an occupation that involves skills you particularly enjoy using, you may sometimes need to intentionally develop skills that you lack—and that may even be outside of your comfort zone. In CHAPTER 11 you will learn about the numerous opportunities available for gaining experience and skills that are relevant to your career path. See ACTIVITIES 3.3, 3.4, and 3.5 to explore skills you may need to improve, specialized knowledge you may need to obtain, and personal attributes you may wish to develop.

DANNY'S STORY

By the end of his freshman year, Danny had his heart set on becoming a fundraiser for nonprofit organizations, a career that he had considered off and on since high school. Because he wanted to make sure that he would have the skills needed to break in to this occupation after graduating from college, Danny began to research it in more depth. Unfortunately, upon interviewing several fundraising professionals, he was horrified to learn that public speaking—a skill which Danny thought he lacked altogether, and which he also found frightening—was one of the occasional job requirements. Dejected, Danny took a mental vacation from thinking about his career development. But several months later, he realized that, despite his reluctance toward public speaking, he was still enthusiastic about the field. Danny decided that come what may, he would not only become a good public speaker, but learn to enjoy it too. He joined two campus organizations that offered regular speaking opportunities, and also committed to attending a local Toastmaster's group, which helps members develop their public speaking skills. It was slow going at first, and several times he considered switching to a different career path. But it wasn't long before Danny started receiving compliments from audience members. One told him he was "a natural" public speaker, and another told him that it was the most effective speech he'd ever heard. Danny realized that even though he was still anxious about giving speeches, his skills were quickly improving. He also realized that he was enjoying the process of his pre-speech anxiety metamorphosing into excitement by the end of a speech. As a result of his newly-developed skills, Danny's confidence blossomed. He now knew that there was nothing that could stand between him and his chosen profession.

CONCLUSION

By assessing your current skills and comparing them to the skills you will need to enter and succeed in the career of your choice, you can get a head start on life after college by making a conscious effort to improve the skills you have and develop new ones as needed.

Once you know your skills—the things you do well—you can begin to make connections between your skills and your interests—the things you enjoy. With these new puzzle pieces in place, you may find that certain skills logically and naturally connect to certain interests, which will make the discovery of a satisfying major and career that much more likely.

CHAPTER 3

ACTIVITIES

ACTIVITY 3.1 **IDENTIFY YOUR SKILLS**

Identify your skills by placing a checkmark in the box next to each skill that you have used in any work or academic setting. Think carefully before concluding that you have never used a skill.

- ☐ **Administer:** perform day-to-day tasks such as maintaining information files and processing paperwork

- ☐ **Advise / Counsel / Consult:** provide guidance, support, or expert advice to individuals or groups

- ☐ **Analyze:** identify the underlying principles, reasons, or facts by breaking down information or data into separate parts

- ☐ **Appraise / Assess:** estimate or evaluate the value, importance, or quality of an object or real estate

- ☐ **Assemble:** put or piece together parts of an object or information

- ☐ **Assist / Treat:** provide personal assistance, medical attention, emotional support, or other care to others such as coworkers, customers, or patients

- ☐ **Budget:** determine how money will be spent to get the work done, and account for these expenditures

- ☐ **Build a team:** encourage and build mutual trust, respect, and cooperation among team members

- ☐ **Build relationships:** develop constructive and cooperative working relationships with others, and maintain them over time

- ☐ **Calculate:** use mathematics to solve problems

- ☐ **Canvass:** go through a region to solicit votes, subscriptions, or orders; conduct a survey of public opinion

- ☐ **Coach / Mentor:** serve as a trusted counselor, teacher, or guide by identifying the developmental needs of others and helping them to improve their knowledge or skills

- ☐ **Collaborate:** work together with others on a common project

- ☐ **Collect:** call and obtain payment for monies due; take in donations

- ☐ **Communicate:** provide information to supervisors, coworkers, or subordinates

- ☐ **Conceive:** form or develop an idea in the mind

- ☐ **Construct:** make or form by putting together materials and parts; create by organizing ideas or arguments

- ☐ **Coordinate:** adjust actions in relation to others' actions

- ☐ **Coordinate a team:** get members of a group to work together to accomplish tasks

- ☐ **Correspond:** communicate with others in writing

- ☐ **Create:** develop new ideas or products

☐ **Decide:** analyze information, consider the relative costs and benefits of potential actions, and choose the most appropriate action

☐ **Design:** plan and fashion the form and structure of an object, work of art, or decorative scheme

☐ **Dispense / Distribute:** pass out, ship, or deliver information or goods to individuals or retailers

☐ **Display:** spread out merchandise for viewing by the public, present objects for a public exhibition

☐ **Draft / Lay out / Specify:** provide documentation, detailed instructions, drawings, or specifications to tell others about how devices, parts, equipment, or structures are to be constructed, assembled, maintained, or used

☐ **Edit:** direct the preparation of a publication; revise or correct a manuscript; assemble components of a video or audio presentation by deleting, arranging, or splicing

☐ **Entertain / Perform:** show hospitality or engage the attention of others

☐ **Estimate:** make an approximate judgment of sizes, distances, and quantities; determine time, costs, resources, or materials needed to perform a work activity

☐ **Facilitate:** assist and support a group of people to function effectively toward the achievement of an outcome

☐ **Inspect:** inspect equipment, structures, or materials to identify the cause of errors or other problems or defects

☐ **Install:** install equipment, machines, wiring, or programs to meet specifications

☐ **Interpret / Explain:** translate or explain what information means and how it can be used, in terms that can be easily understood

☐ **Learn:** assimilate new knowledge or skill for both current and future problem solving and decision making

☐ **Listen:** give full attention to what other people are saying, taking time to understand the points being made, asking questions as appropriate, and not interrupting at inappropriate times

☐ **Maintain:** perform routine maintenance on equipment and determine when and what kind of maintenance is needed

☐ **Manage materials:** obtain and see to the appropriate use of equipment, facilities, and materials needed to do certain work

☐ **Manage time:** manage one's own time and the time of others

☐ **Measure:** ascertain dimensions, quantity, or capacity by comparison with a standard

☐ **Mediate / Handle complaints:** resolve and settle grievances, conflicts, and complaints

☐ **Monitor:** monitor and assess the performance of yourself, others, organizations, machines, or the environment to detect or assess problems, make improvements, or take corrective action

☐ **Motivate:** provide guidance and encouragement to others

☐ **Move / Handle:** use hands and arms in handling, positioning, and moving materials

☐ **Negotiate:** bring others together and attempt to reconcile differences

☐ **Observe:** observe, receive, and otherwise obtain information from all relevant sources

☐ **Operate:** control operations of equipment or systems

☐ **Organize / Plan:** develop specific goals and plans to prioritize, organize, and accomplish your work

☐ **Perform physical activity:** perform physical activities that require considerable use of your arms and legs and moving your whole body, such as climbing, lifting, balancing, walking, stooping, and handling of materials

☐ **Persuade:** persuade others to change their minds or behavior

☐ **Present:** show or offer something to an audience

☐ **Process / Audit:** compile, categorize, calculate, audit, or verify information or data

☐ **Program:** write computer programs for various purposes

☐ **Project / Predict:** calculate, estimate, or forecast a future situation or event based on present data or trends

☐ **Promote / Publicize:** encourage the sales or acceptance of a product or service through advertising or by notifying the public, contribute to the growth of an organization or cause

☐ **Protect:** defend or guard a person, place, or object from loss, injury, or danger

☐ **Recruit / Interview:** recruit, interview, select, and hire employees

☐ **Repair:** repair electronic and/or mechanical devices or systems using the needed tools

☐ **Represent:** act for or on behalf of a person, group, or organization

☐ **Research:** search for facts or information in a systematic manner

☐ **Review:** write a critique of a book, drama, or musical performance

☐ **Schedule:** schedule events, programs, and activities, as well as the work of others

☐ **Select equipment:** determine the kind of tools and/or equipment needed to do a job

☐ **Select learning strategies:** select and use training/instructional methods and procedures appropriate for the situation when learning or teaching

☐ **Sell:** convince others to buy merchandise/goods or to otherwise change their minds or actions

☐ **Serve:** serve customers in restaurants and stores, and receive clients or guests

☐ **Set up:** prepare a physical space for a particular purpose or event

☐ **Sketch:** represent, describe, or portray roughly or briefly

☐ **Solve problems:** identify problems and review relevant information to develop and evaluate options and implement solutions

☐ **Speak (in public):** talk to small and large groups to convey information effectively

☐ **Strategize:** establish long-range objectives and specify the actions to achieve them

☐ **Supervise / Manage:** motivate, develop, and direct people as they work

☐ **Teach / Instruct:** identify educational needs of others, develop educational or training programs or classes, and teach or instruct them

☐ **Think critically:** use logic and reasoning to identify the strengths and weaknesses of alternative solutions, conclusions, or approaches to problems

☐ **Transcribe / Record:** enter, transcribe, record, or maintain information in written or electronic form

☐ **Translate:** restate words from one language into another

☐ **Troubleshoot:** determine causes of errors and decide what to do about them

☐ **Understand written information:** understand written work-related documents

☐ **Update:** keep up-to-date technically and apply new knowledge to your job

☐ **Write:** communicate effectively in writing as appropriate for the needs of the audience

ACTIVITY 3.2 **IDENTIFY ENJOYABLE SKILLS**

Look through the skills you checked off in ACTIVITY 3.1. Write up to 10 skills that you enjoy using the most.

Collabor

Listen

Lear

Corresp

ACTIVITY 3.3 **IDENTIFY SKILLS TO IMPROVE**

You may wish to acquire additional proficiency in certain skills that you find interesting or potentially useful in any career. Or you may have a specific career in mind already and realize that you need to develop certain skills in order to be successful at it. Look through all the skills in ACTIVITY 3.1—both the ones you checked off and the ones you didn't. Write up to 10 skills that you _don't currently have but would like to learn_, or that you _do currently have but would like to improve_.

_A_

Public

Organize

Budget

Motivate

See CHAPTER 11 to develop a plan for acquiring these skills.

ACTIVITY 3.4 **CONSIDER WHAT SPECIALIZED KNOWLEDGE IS NEEDED**

What specialized knowledge might be needed in the following careers?

- Graphic Designer
- Neurosurgeon
- Software Developer
- High School History Teacher
- Attorney

ACTIVITY 3.5 **ASSESS YOUR PERSONAL ATTRIBUTES**

Check off which "personal attributes" you possess or that describe you, and write notes about those you'd like to develop or improve.

Describes Me	Attribute	Improvement Strategies
	Compassionate	
	Creative	
	Decisive	
	Dedicated / Committed	
	Detail-oriented	
	Determined	
	Diplomatic	
	Empathetic	

Describes Me	Attribute	Improvement Strategies
	Encouraging / Supportive	
	Energetic	
	Enthusiastic	
	Ethical	
	Fair	
	Flexible / Adaptable	
	Friendly / Personable	
	Generous	
	Honest	
	Integrity	
	Mindful	
	Motivated	
	Open-minded	
	Organized	
	Outgoing	
	Patient	

Describes Me	Attribute	Improvement Strategies
	Polite	
	Positive	
	Professional / Businesslike	
	Punctual	
	Quiet	
	Respectful of diversity	
	Responsible / Reliable	
	Risk taker	
	Self-confident	
	Self-disciplined	
	Sense of humor	
	Service-oriented	
	Strong work ethic	
	Task-focused	
	Warm	
	Willing to learn	

SUMMARY & KEY POINTS

- There are three types of skills: transferable skills, specialized knowledge, and personal attributes.

- Knowing and intentionally developing your skills will help you to find a more satisfying occupation and improve your potential for success in it.

INTERESTS

"The supreme accomplishment is to blur the line between work and play."

ARNOLD TOYNBEE, HISTORIAN

INTRODUCTION

It's a simple question: What are you interested in? Your answer might lie in your leisure life and what you like to do in your spare time, as it does for many people. But how do you carry your interests into the world of work? Ideally, as Toynbee's quote suggests, your leisure and work interests will overlap so you will be deeply engaged and satisfied with your job activities. However, some of your top leisure interests may not be easily fulfilled in your job.

Learning Objectives

» Understand Holland's six interest themes from his theory of occupational interests

» Identify your interest themes and how they align with work environments

» Recognize potential interactions of interest themes, and how combinations of interests can be present in work environments

WORK VS. PLAY

Jonathan is a passionate adventurer. In his spare time, he enjoys outdoor recreational activities. This is why he chose to live near the mountains, where there are opportunities for mountain biking, rock climbing, and most important, bungee jumping.

Jonathan loves to bungee jump more than any other recreational activity. However, he knew throughout college that his number one passion wouldn't bring in the big bucks, as no one will pay him to bungee jump. Jonathan decided to pursue a degree with a major in Recreational Sports Management.

(continued)

WORK VS. PLAY *(continued)*

With his current job at a national park, he gets to work outdoors, maintain beautiful landscapes, and participate in leisure activities at a discount. Although his number one interest isn't part of his daily work, he found a way to enjoy his work on a daily basis. One day, he might open his own bungee jumping business and get paid to teach others his favorite hobby!

Knowing your interests will be a big factor in the choice you make for your major and career. Among the other elements of your Personal Career Profile, your interests can guide your major and career decisions by steering you toward what keeps you engaged and feeling passionate. This chapter will help you define your career interest themes and types of work environments that may match your interests.

THE ORIGIN OF YOUR INTERESTS

Interests are a completely different category than skills. For example, imagine you took piano lessons as a child, and everyone complimented you on how wonderfully you played. But you absolutely hated your lessons, practicing, and playing piano in general. You may have skills in learning music and hand-eye coordination, but you are not passionate about pursuing music performance as a career. Remember that having a skill does not necessarily mean you are interested in using it in a career, and a career interest does not have to reflect your current set of skills. Of course, it is certainly possible to develop skills that will allow you to pursue one of your interests.

The piano example demonstrates a reaction to external influences, as you learned about in CHAPTER 1. Young adults are often influenced by people and situations around them. As a new college student, you may have had few opportunities to make important choices for yourself. Your decisions up until now have likely been influenced by external factors that may have impeded the discovery of your true interests. In addition, exposure to a variety of interests and subjects may have been limited. As you reach adulthood, more decisions will be yours to make. As you begin the major and career decision-making process, be aware of what's influencing your interests. For more information on decision making, see CHAPTER 9.

HOLLAND'S THEORY OF OCCUPATIONAL INTERESTS

In 1973, John Holland developed a theory of interest themes represented by the six points on a hexagon. Holland proposed that people can be categorized into one, or likely a combination, of these six theme areas, and that work environments can also be categorized into the same theme areas. Therefore, work environments would be populated heavily by people whose interests align with that particular interest theme. Because people and work environments align, Holland believed people would seek out types of work that match their own interest themes, and therefore be more satisfied and engaged. Holland's theory has been incorporated into several interest inventories, including the Strong Interest Inventory® instrument.

Theme Labels

» Don't take the theme names too literally. Holland's definitions of the themes are different from the common meanings of these terms.

HOLLAND'S HEXAGON

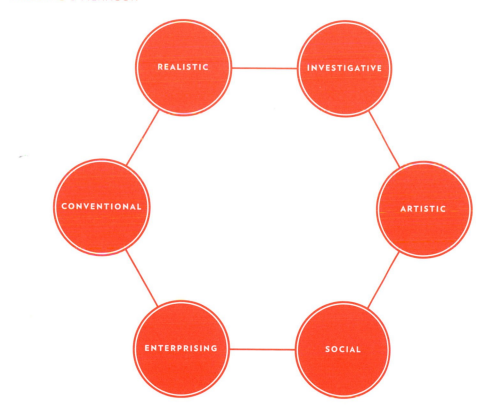

REALISTIC

INVESTIGATIVE

CONVENTIONAL

ARTISTIC

ENTERPRISING

SOCIAL

THE SIX THEMES

The theme areas of Holland's hexagon include: Realistic, Investigative, Artistic, Social, Enterprising, and Conventional. The first letter of each theme is often used to represent it (RIASEC). The combination and sequence of a person's interest themes is known as their *Holland Theme Code*.

Realistic (The Doers)

People whose interests align with a Realistic theme are motivated by using their physical skill. They usually enjoy hands-on, mechanical, or outdoor activities. Fixing, repairing, and working with machinery are common activities associated with this theme. This interest theme involves using tools, equipment, physical abilities, and manual dexterity. Realistic people like to spend time outdoors and often participate in athletics and adventurous activities. They like to have clear lines of authority and tangible results from the work they complete. They prefer concrete problems rather than abstract complication, and prefer action over thought. The term "Realistic" does not imply that those without this theme in their code are "unrealistic" in the usual meaning of the word.

Realistic People May Be:

- Action-oriented
- Concrete thinkers
- Constructive
- Drawn to the outdoors
- Hands-on
- Mechanical
- Observant
- Physical
- Practical

Realistic Environments Often Involve:

- Adventurous activities
- Athletics
- Building things
- Clear lines of authority
- Fixing or repairing things
- Manufacturing
- Operating machinery
- Using physical strength
- Using tools with precision

Investigative (The Thinkers)

People whose interests align with an Investigative theme are motivated by analyzing. Investigative people may be drawn to observation, conducting research, or developing new theories and models. They usually prefer to work independently in an unstructured environment. This theme involves using critical thought to solve complex problems, as well as compiling and analyzing data. Investigative people often enjoy working in intellectual, research-oriented environments, possibly in a scientific lab or in academia.

Investigative People May Be:

- Academic
- Complex
- Independent
- Intellectual
- Scientific
- Self-motivated
- Task-oriented
- Theoretical
- Unstructured

Investigative Environments Often Involve:

- Analyzing
- Computer work
- Critical thinking
- Laboratory work
- Mathematics
- Research
- Solving complex problems
- Thinking and writing about new ideas
- Working with data

Artistic (The Creators)

People whose interests align with an Artistic theme are motivated by expressing their creativity. Artistic people enjoy communicating their individuality and unique ideas. They prefer working independently where they can express themselves in a distinct way. The Artistic theme involves coming up with new ideas in an unstructured environment. Artistic people may enjoy creating artwork, writing, designing, performing, or many other creative activities. The Artistic theme is also associated with the appreciation of artistic works. In addition, Artistic people tend to be drawn to flexible, aesthetically pleasing environments. In this context, the theme "Artistic" indicates having creative interests, not necessarily doing or making actual artwork.

Artistic People May Be:

- Creative
- Dramatic
- Flexible
- Imaginative
- Intuitive
- Musical
- Non-conforming
- Self-expressive
- Unique

Artistic Environments Often Involve:

- Creating artwork
- Designing
- Expressing individuality
- Music and instruments
- Performing
- Unstructured activities
- Using ideas to create something
- Working independently
- Writing or composing

Social (The Helpers)

People whose interests align with a Social theme are motivated by helping others. Social people are drawn to activities that involve helping or encouraging. They prefer to work in environments that are supportive and relationship-based. The Social theme often involves working collaboratively with others to achieve goals. Social people may enjoy teaching, counseling, or guiding others. They often thrive on group work, either as a team member or as a leader. Although the term "social" may imply an outgoing personality, in this context the theme "Social" simply indicates an interest in helping others.

Social People May Be:

- Cooperative
- Empathetic
- Friendly
- Generous
- Helpful
- Humanistic
- Idealistic
- Insightful
- Understanding

Social Environments Often Involve:

- Counseling
- Helping
- Listening
- Nurturing or healing
- Social service activities
- Supporting
- Teaching
- Volunteer activities
- Working in a group

Enterprising (The Persuaders)

People whose interests align with an Enterprising theme are motivated by persuading and influencing others. Enterprising people often enjoy taking on leadership roles and debating ideas. They prefer to work in environments that are competitive and fast-paced. The Enterprising theme often involves selling, taking risks, and business-related activities. Enterprising people often enjoy managing people and projects, competition, and promoting their ideas. Like the Social theme, this theme also relates to working with people, but with an emphasis on leading others, not necessarily a helping motivation.

Enterprising People May Be:

- Ambitious
- Assertive
- Competitive
- Driven to succeed
- Energetic
- Influential
- Leadership-oriented
- Resilient
- Risk-takers

Enterprising Environments Often Involve:

- Business and corporate activities
- Debating
- Directing others
- Entertaining
- Entrepreneurship
- Managing people and projects
- Political activities
- Promotional activities and marketing
- Speaking in front of large groups

Conventional (The Organizers)

People whose interests align with a Conventional theme are motivated by organizing information. Conventional people typically enjoy working with computers and managing data. They prefer to work in environments that are structured, organized, and hierarchical. The Conventional theme often involves working with computer systems and databases. Conventional people tend to be drawn to practical, organized activities. Keep in mind that the term "Conventional" does not imply that those without this theme in their code are "unconventional" in the usual meaning of the word.

Conventional People May Be:

- Accurate
- Conscientious
- Detail-oriented
- Efficient
- Organized
- Patient
- Practical
- Structured
- Systematic

Conventional Environments Often Involve:

- Accounting and numbers
- Budgeting
- Business and office activities
- Data management
- Making charts and graphs
- Operating computers
- Record keeping
- Technical activities
- Writing reports

YOUR HOLLAND THEME CODE

Now that you've read about the different interest themes, you may have noticed that one or several of the themes sound(s) interesting to you. On the list below, rank the interest themes in terms of how they align with your own interests:

Rank	Interest Theme
	Realistic (Doers)
	Investigative (Thinkers)
	Artistic (Creators)
	Social (Helpers)
	Enterprising (Persuaders)
	Conventional (Organizers)

Your Holland Theme Code		
1	2	3

Your top three ranked interest themes are collectively known as your Holland Theme Code. Once you've estimated your Holland Theme Code, you may want to verify it by thinking about your past activities and the themes that motivated you. See AC-TIVITY 4.2 for help in identifying your best-fit theme code.

The Ranking of Your Interest Themes

The letters of your Holland Theme Code may display a dynamic relationship in the way you carry out your work. Some believe that the first letter in your Holland Theme Code will largely determine your career choice, since the majority of your interests likely fall into that category. The first theme is sometimes referred to as your "passion," or what you're drawn to do with your life. The other two themes may indicate how you would like to pursue your interest area of choice.

NONPROFIT DIRECTOR: **SAE**

Elizabeth's Holland Theme Code is SAE. She wasn't surprised that she selected Social (S) as her top theme, because she is passionate about helping other people. She finds engagement and satisfaction by giving her time and energy to improve others' lives. As a dream job, Elizabeth has always wanted to begin her own food pantry that provides healthy food to low income families.

Her other two themes are Artistic (A) and Enterprising (E). Perhaps Elizabeth could pursue her passion for working in a Social environment while connecting creative and leadership activities to accomplish and carry out her work. For example, she may display her Artistic theme by developing new and unique ways to market her services to families in the community. She may also incorporate her Enterprising theme by leading groups and committees at the food pantry, and presenting their annual report to the board of directors.

See ACTIVITY 4.3 to apply the concept of theme dynamics to your own Holland Theme Code.

Theme Proximity

Holland strategically placed the theme locations on the hexagon to indicate similarity among the themes. Themes that are closely related are adjacent to each other, while themes that are less related are across from each other on the diagram. For example, a Realistic theme is more closely related to Investigative and Conventional, and less related to the Social theme. Furthermore, proximity also indicates that if your themes are adjacent, you are more likely to find a career that includes two or three of your interest themes.

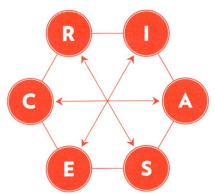

Elizabeth's Holland Theme Code described how adjacent themes may interact with each other. Many theme codes will include themes from points near each other on the hexagon, but some do not. While there may be fewer occupations with diagonal themes, it is still possible to target your greatest areas of interest and incorporate them into your job. Dr. Henry's code exemplifies how diagonal themes may be displayed.

PROFESSOR OF BIOLOGY: **IES**

Dr. Henry is a tenured biology professor at a large university. His career is focused on research, writing, and data. His top-level interest area has remained an Investigative (I) theme since he was a young Ph.D. student. However, his interests also guide him toward sharing his expertise with students in helpful ways.

He loves expressing his Enterprising (E) interest by leading large lecture classes and providing knowledge and insight to hundreds of young students. He also owns a consulting business outside of his university work, which allows him to express his business and leadership interests. In addition, he displays his Social (S) interest by devoting free time to helping students with questions about the class material. He is always concerned about each student's progress in his classes, and is willing to give his time to make sure they are learning and understanding the material.

I Have Too Many Interests!

Some may find it difficult to narrow their interest themes down to three to form a Holland Theme Code. What if you have so many interests, you can't fit them all into a three-letter sequence encompassing everything that drives you? What if you have positive responses to many or all of the interest themes? Think about why it's difficult for you to define your top interest areas. Perhaps you equate "disliking" something with negativity. As mentioned earlier, you may define your world externally and want to please others. Or, defining your interests may make you feel like you are excluding other options or pinning yourself down to a certain career field. However, some people truly do have a diversity of interests and would like to incorporate as many themes into their daily work as possible.

I'm Not Interested In Anything!

On the other hand, some may find it difficult to define any of their interests. What if you've read the descriptions of each theme, and none of them sound interesting to you? It could be that you have narrowly defined interests that are not necessarily exemplified by the given interest themes.

However, there are a variety of common reasons why interests may be hard to articulate. Different cultures view the world of work differently, so your personal background may influence your responses to the interest themes. If you are externally defined, your interest choices may be in response to family or peer pressure about what you "should" be interested in. A limited knowledge of the world of work can also play a role in defining work interests. In some cases, an inability to define interests may indicate decision-making difficulties (see CHAPTER 9), fear of commitment, indifference, low self-esteem, or depression. If you feel like any of these issues are impacting your career decision making, your campus career or counseling centers are available to provide guidance.

CONCLUSION

Along with values, skills, and personality, defining your interests will be tremendously useful when brainstorming major and career options to research. In addition, knowing your interest themes can help you choose activities and organizations to become involved with outside of the classroom. After identifying your themes, reflect on activities that will bring you energy, excitement, and a desire to learn more. Use these activities to gain experiences and build skills that will help you in the eventual job search. Interests tend to change over time as you are exposed to different experiences and environments, so re-evaluate your interest themes often and seek out opportunities that are engaging and satisfying to you.

After reading about values, skills, and interests, you might be starting to see connections among these elements. The next chapter will discuss personality preferences and further contribute to the big picture of your Personal Career Profile. Each element is a piece of the larger puzzle, which can be used to guide your research and decision making as you cycle through your career development.

CHAPTER 4

ACTIVITIES

ACTIVITY 4.1   **BRAINSTORM INTERESTS OF FAMOUS PEOPLE**

Brainstorm famous people or characters who have interests aligning with each of the interest themes. For example, Albert Einstein might come to mind for the Investigative theme. After brainstorming famous peoples' interests, ask yourself why you chose those people for each theme. What motivates their interests?

ACTIVITY 4.2   **IDENTIFY YOUR BEST-FIT THEME CODE**

Reflect on what you're passionate about. Make a list of clubs, organizations, volunteer work, leisure activities, sports, academic subjects, or classes that give you energy, excitement, or a desire to learn more. Which Holland Theme(s) do each of these activities align with? What motivated you to participate in these activities? Do you see any patterns?

ACTIVITY 4.3   **CONSIDER THEME DYNAMICS**

Using Elizabeth's story (p. 57) as an example, consider your own Holland Theme Code and how it applies to the concept of theme dynamics. Cite examples of how you would like your interest areas to interact with each other in your ideal work environment.

SUMMARY & KEY POINTS

- Holland's theory of occupational interests states that both people's interests and work environments can be categorized as combinations and sequences of six themes: Realistic, Investigative, Artistic, Social, Enterprising, and Conventional.

- Interactions of theme codes can be displayed in different ways in work environments.

- Interest theme clarity can be affected by external influences.

PERSONALITY PREFERENCES

"The privilege of a lifetime is being who you are."

JOSEPH CAMPBELL, MYTHOLOGIST

INTRODUCTION

Now that you've explored your values, skills, and interests, the final piece of the Personal Career Profile to consider is personality. Personality refers to a pattern of mental, emotional, physical, and behavioral characteristics of an individual. People are naturally drawn to work environments and career areas that align with their personality patterns, or preferences. Furthermore, there are potential strengths and challenges associated with personality preferences. If you can identify your preferences, you are more likely to capitalize on your strengths, confront your challenges, and make decisions accordingly.

Knowing your personality preferences will not only help you in making career decisions, but also in other areas of life. Often, personality differentiation is used in creating teams in work settings, assigning tasks, and organizing responsibilities. Information about personality can provide insight into personal relationships and interaction among people. Understanding the opposites of your preferences can also promote acceptance and appreciation of others. Additionally, one of the most important elements of your personality type is the impact it has on your decision-making style. (For more on decision-making styles as they relate to personality, see CHAPTER 9.)

Learning Objectives

» Understand personality preferences as defined by Carl Jung and the Myers-Briggs Type Indicator® (MBTI®) instrument

» Identify your four personality preferences and begin to think about your preferred work environments

» Assess your selected personality type for potential strengths and challenges related to career decision making

There are four elements of personality, and much of this chapter will be dedicated to defining the four personality elements (and eight corresponding indicators) used in the Myers-Briggs Type Indicator instrument, and to deepen your understanding of your personality type. Please be advised that this information is not a substitute for a personality assessment, as this chapter will not provide the same depth of information or research data on personality preferences. If you think you might benefit from taking a personality assessment such as the MBTI instrument, see your campus career center.

JUNG'S PSYCHOLOGICAL TYPE THEORY AND THE MBTI® INSTRUMENT

In 1921, psychiatrist Carl Jung unveiled his theory of psychological type to explain the normal differences between healthy people. He proposed that people naturally have preferences to use their minds in certain ways, resulting in patterns of behavior, also known as personality type. Jung's theory was researched further by Katharine Briggs and Isabel Briggs Myers. This mother-daughter team developed an instrument that allowed the public to understand and apply Jung's theory. The Myers-Briggs Type Indicator instrument was first published in the 1940s, and continues to be tested, revised, and validated today. The MBTI instrument is one of the most widely used personality assessments in educational, work, and counseling settings.

The MBTI instrument uses responses to categorize respondents into one of 16 personality types. The instrument reports respondents' preferences in four areas:

1. Where you focus your energy and attention
2. How you take in information
3. How you make decisions
4. How you deal with the outer world

NATURAL PREFERENCES

Personality preferences are the natural tendencies that make you more comfortable in one situation over another. Consider the way you cross your arms. Try folding your arms in a comfortable position. How long does it take you to do so? How much thought goes into it? Next, fold your arms with the opposite arm on the outside. What differences do you notice between the first arm cross and the second? Were there differences in speed? Comfort? Concentration? Self-awareness?

You naturally have a preference for crossing your arms with one arm on the outside. But when you're asked to go about doing this activity in a non-preferred way, it takes more effort and thought to get it right. The same is true for personality preferences and work. Working in an environment that does not complement your natural preferences may require much more energy for you to be comfortable and to succeed. However, with practice and experience, we can certainly develop behaviors out of our natural type. We can, and do, operate out of type in many situations, and as we grow, opposite preferences may become more developed.

THE FOUR DICHOTOMIES

As you read through each of the following preference descriptions, try to identify which one in each dichotomous pair best describes your own preferences. Note that the bold letter for each preference is often used to represent it. Remember to select your true preferences, not how you think others perceive you or your behavior.

Extraversion	**OR**	**I**ntroversion
Sensing	**OR**	I**N**tuition
Thinking	**OR**	**F**eeling
Judging	**OR**	**P**erceiving

» Extraversion should not be confused with the term "extroversion." Extroversion is associated with being outgoing, but Extraversion (the personality preference) simply means you are energized by the outside world.

» The term Introversion does not necessarily indicate a shy or reserved personality, but simply an inner source of energy and attention.

Focus of Energy and Attention: Extraversion and Introversion

Your first personality preference is determined by where you get your energy, and where you focus your attention. People who prefer **Extraversion** tend to get their energy from the outside world, by interacting and communicating with others. They focus their attention outwardly, and tend to have a breadth of interests.

Those who prefer **Introversion** tend to get their energy from their inner thoughts and reflections. They focus their attention inwardly and tend to have a depth of interests. Introversion is associated with reflecting on thoughts, memories, and feelings.

Extraversion	Introversion
Attuned to external environment	Drawn to their inner world
Prefer to communicate by talking	Prefer to communicate in writing
Work out ideas by talking them through	Work out ideas by reflecting on them
Learn best through doing or discussing	Learn best by reflection, mental "practice"
Have broad interests	Focus in depth on their interests
Sociable and expressive	Private and contained
Readily take initiative in work and relationships	Take initiative when the situation or issue is very important to them

Work Environment

Preferences for Extraversion or Introversion may be displayed in work environments in the following ways:

Extraversion:

• Like variety and action

• Enjoy interacting with people

• Develop ideas through discussion

• Learn new tasks by talking and doing

• Interested in how other people do their work

Introversion:

• Like quiet for concentration

• Enjoy focusing on a project or task

• Develop ideas internally

• Learn new tasks by reading and reflecting

• Enjoy working alone with no interruptions

Taking In Information: Sensing and Intuition

The second personality preference is determined by how you take in information. People with a **Sensing** preference take in information through details, specifics, and experiences. They tend to notice the observable, concrete details of a situation and focus on the physical realities, rather than a larger picture. They often use their five senses, taking in information in a descriptive way through sight, sound, and touch.

Those with a preference for **Intuition** take in information through possibilities, associations, and their imagination. They tend to visualize the big picture, not necessarily the details that generate it. When taking in information, they see possibilities, patterns, connections, and ideas. Notice that the Intuition preference uses "N" as its indicator, simply because "I" has already been used to represent Introversion.

Sensing	Intuition
Oriented to present realities	Oriented to future possibilities
Factual and concrete	Imaginative and verbally creative
Focus on what is real and actual	Focus on patterns and meanings in data
Observe and remember specifics	Remember specifics when they relate to a pattern
Build carefully and thoroughly toward conclusions	Move quickly to conclusions, follow hunches
Understand ideas and theories through practical applications	Want to clarify ideas and theories before putting them into practice
Trust experience	Trust inspiration

Work Environment

Preferences for Sensing or Intuition may be displayed in work environments in the following ways:

Sensing:

- Focus on immediate issues
- Provide a realistic and practical perspective
- Like to perfect standard ways to do things by fine tuning
- Build to conclusions by collecting facts
- Draw on their own and others' experience

Intuition:

- Follow their inspirations
- Provide connections and meanings
- Like solving new, complex problems
- Start with the big picture, fill in the facts
- Prefer change, new ways of doing things

Clarification of Terminology

» A preference for Thinking does not indicate an "emotionless" temperament, and a preference for Feeling does not indicate less reasoning ability.

Making Decisions: Thinking and Feeling

The third personality preference is determined by how you make decisions. People with a **Thinking** preference prefer to make decisions based on logical consequences. They reason out the possible choices when making a decision, and come to an objective conclusion. They tend to stick to principles and guidelines when deciding on a course of action.

Those with a preference for **Feeling** make decisions based on personal values and compassion. When making a choice, they use subjective reasoning; they consider the consequences of their choice to all others involved, and the impact it might have. They use their person-centered values and the unique situations of others to guide their decision making.

Thinking	Feeling
Analytical	Empathetic
Use cause-and-effect reasoning	Guided by personal values
Solve problems with logic	Assess impacts of decisions on people
Strive for an objective standard of truth	Strive for harmony and positive interactions
Reasonable	Compassionate
Can be "tough-minded"	May appear "tender-hearted"
Fair by treating everyone equally	Fair by treating everyone individually

Work Environment

Preferences for Thinking or Feeling may be displayed in work environments in the following ways:

Thinking:

- Focus on tasks
- Use logical analysis to understand and decide
- Want mutual respect and fairness among colleagues
- Are firm-minded, can give criticism when appropriate
- Apply principles consistently

Feeling:

- Focus on people's interactions
- Use values to understand and decide
- Want harmony and support among colleagues
- Are empathetic, prefer to accommodate and reach consensus
- Apply values consistently

Dealing with the Outer World: Judging and Perceiving

The final personality preference is determined by how you deal with the outer world and the need for order in your life. People with a **Judging** preference tend to seek structure and organization in their daily life. They like to accomplish tasks and projects in a timely manner, while sticking to an established plan.

Those with a preference for **Perceiving** tend to seek flexibility and spontaneity in their daily life. They prefer to have more openness in their plans and tend to feel restricted with a set schedule. They are comfortable adapting to a changing environment.

Clarification of Terminology

» A preference for Judging does not indicate "judgmental," only a need for order, in this context.

» A preference for Perceiving does not indicate "perceptiveness."

Judging	Perceiving
Scheduled	Spontaneous
Organized	Flexible
Systematic	Casual
Methodical	Open-ended
Make short- and long-term plans	Adapt, change course
Like to have things decided	Like things open to change
Try to avoid last-minute stresses	Feel energized by last-minute pressures

Work Environment

Preferences for Judging or Perceiving may be displayed in work environments in the following ways:

Judging:

- Want to plan their work and follow the plan
- Like to get things settled and finished
- Feel supported by structure and schedules
- Reach closure by deciding quickly
- Focus on timely completion of a project

Perceiving:

- Want to have flexibility in their work
- Like to be spontaneous
- Feel restricted by structure and schedules
- Leave things open as long as possible
- Focus on enjoying the process

ESTIMATE YOUR PERSONALITY TYPE

One of the preferences in each pair will likely seem more comfortable to you. Select one preference from each pair, the sequence of which makes up your self-estimated personality type, indicated by the corresponding letters. For example, an ISFJ has preferences for Introversion, Sensing, Feeling, and Judging.

What is your self-estimated personality type?			
E/I	S/N	T/F	J/P

The table on pp. 72-73 provides a brief description of all 16 personality types. Read the description of your self-estimated type or reported type. If the description doesn't appear to accurately describe you, you may want to read descriptions of other types to verify. For example, if you self-estimated as an ENFP, but you weren't completely sure about the F, read the descriptions for both ENFP and ENTP to gain clarity.

DISCOVER YOUR BEST-FIT TYPE

For some people, the identification of preferences is obvious. But for many others, self-estimating a type can be challenging. If selecting a type or a set of preferences is difficult for you, there are strategies to help you with the process. If you have taken the MBTI instrument, compare your self-estimated type to your reported type. It's okay if there are differences. It could be that you were not in a relaxed state of mind when you took the assessment. Or, you may have self-estimated how others see you, not necessarily your true preferences. Perhaps you are genuinely not yet clear on your preferences, which is common in early adulthood. Remember that we can and do function in all eight areas, but we have one preference from each pair.

If your reported and self-estimated types are not the same, there are resources available to help verify your "best-fit" type. You may want to visit your campus career center to process this information with a career advisor. There are also many books and websites that may assist you in verifying your type. See the list at the end of this chapter for suggested readings. You may also want to reflect on past experiences to identify personality preferences you have displayed. People close to you, such as family and friends, may be able to remind you of experiences that exemplify your preferences.

EXPLORING TYPE DYNAMICS

Your personality type is not simply a sum of its parts, but rather a dynamic system of interrelationships among your preferences. Reading full type descriptions can often be more helpful than analyzing each dichotomy in isolation. Type descriptions can help with exploring type dynamics, another strategy that can help you identify behaviors or preferences that are not quite as obvious.

The concept of type dynamics can seem complex, but the principles are easy to understand. Each person has a set of mental functions that operate as their "heart of type." Your mental functions are the middle two letters of your type: your perception style (Sensing or Intuition) and your decision-making style (Thinking or Feeling). Look back at your self-estimated, reported, or best-fit type.

CHARACTERISTICS FREQUENTLY ASSOCIATED WITH EACH TYPE

Sensing Types

Introverts

ISTJ

Quiet, serious, earn success by thoroughness and dependability. Practical, matter-of-fact, realistic, and responsible. Decide logically what should be done and work toward it steadily, regardless of distractions. Take pleasure in making everything orderly and organized — their work, their home, their life. Value traditions and loyalty.

ISTP

Tolerant and flexible, quiet observers until a problem appears, then act quickly to find workable solutions. Analyze what makes things work and readily get through large amounts of data to isolate the core of practical problems. Interested in cause and effect, organize facts using logical principles, value efficiency.

ISFJ

Quiet, friendly, responsible, and conscientious. Committed and steady in meeting their obligations. Thorough, painstaking, and accurate. Loyal, considerate, notice and remember specifics about people who are important to them, concerned with how others feel. Strive to create an orderly and harmonious environment at work and at home.

ISFP

Quiet, friendly, sensitive, and kind. Enjoy the present moment, what's going on around them. Like to have their own space and to work within their own time frame. Loyal and committed to their values and to people who are important to them. Dislike disagreements and conflicts, do not force their opinions or values on others.

Extraverts

ESTP

Flexible and tolerant, they take a pragmatic approach focused on immediate results. Theories and conceptual explanations bore them — they want to act energetically to solve the problem. Focus on the here-and-now, spontaneous, enjoy each moment that they can be active with others. Enjoy material comforts and style. Learn best through doing.

ESTJ

Practical, realistic, matter-of-fact. Decisive, quickly move to implement decisions. Organize projects and people to get things done, focus on getting results in the most efficient way possible. Take care of routine details. Have a clear set of logical standards, systematically follow them and want others to also. Forceful in implementing their plans.

ESFP

Outgoing, friendly, and accepting. Exuberant lovers of life, people, and material comforts. Enjoy working with others to make things happen. Bring common sense and realistic approach to their work, and make work fun. Flexible and spontaneous, adapt readily to new people and environments. Learn best by trying a new skill with other people.

ESFJ

Warmhearted, conscientious, and cooperative. Want harmony in their environment, work with determination to establish it. Like to work with others to complete tasks accurately and on time. Loyal, follow through even in small matters. Notice what others need in their day-by-day lives and try to provide it. Want to be appreciated for who they are and for what they contribute.

This table only provides descriptions for MBTI types. Types estimated from other sources are not represented in this table.

Characteristics Frequently Associated With Each Type

Intuitive Types

INFJ

Seek meaning and connection in ideas, relationships, and material possessions. Want to understand what motivates people and are insightful about others. Conscientious and committed to their firm values. Develop a clear vision about how best to serve the common good. Organized and decisive in implementing their vision.

INFP

Idealistic, loyal to their values and to people who are important to them. Want an external life that is congruent with their values. Curious, quick to see possibilities, can be catalysts for implementing ideas. Seek to understand people and to help them fulfill their potential. Adaptable, flexible, and accepting unless a value is threatened.

ENFP

Warmly enthusiastic and imaginative. See life as full of possibilities. Make connections between events and information very quickly, and confidently proceed based on the patterns they see. Want a lot of affirmation from others, and readily give appreciation and support. Spontaneous and flexible, often rely on their ability to improvise and their verbal fluency.

ENFJ

Warm, empathetic, responsive, and reponsible. Highly attuned to the emotions, needs, and motivations of others. Find potential in everyone, want to help others fulfill their potential. May act as catalysts for individual and group growth. Loyal, responsive to praise and criticism. Sociable, facilitate others in a group, and provide inspiring leadership.

INTJ

Have original minds and great drive for implementing their ideas and achieving their goals. Quickly see patterns in external events, and develop long-range explanatory perspectives. When committed, organize a job and carry it through. Skeptical and independent, have high standards of competence and performance for themselves and others.

INTP

Seek to develop logical explanations for everything that interests them. Theoretical and abstract, interested more in ideas that in social interaction. Quiet, contained, flexible, and adaptable. Have unusual ability to focus in depth to solve problems in their area of interest. Skeptical, sometimes critical, always analytical.

ENTP

Quick, ingenious, stimulating, alert, and outspoken. Resourceful in solving new and challenging problems. Adept at generating conceptual possibilities and then analyzing them strategically. Good at reading other people. Bored by routine, will seldom do the same thing the same way, apt to turn to one new interest after another.

ENTJ

Frank, decisive, assume leadership readily. Quickly see illogical and inefficient procedures and policies, develop and implement comprehensive systems to solve organizational problems. Enjoy long-term planning and goal setting. Usually well informed, well read, enjoy expanding their knowledge and passing it on to others. Forceful in presenting their ideas.

What is your mental function pair?	
S or N	T or F

Everyone has a favorite function (a dominant function). You use your favorite function in your preferred world (either Extraversion or Introversion). Your dominant function could be compared to the captain of a ship, guiding and directing your course and consciousness. This dominant function is the first function that is fully developed in your life, since you are most comfortable using this function in your most comfortable world (outer or inner world). Your second favorite function (the auxiliary function) balances out your dominant function, and is displayed in your less preferred world (outer or inner). Your two favorite functions (dominant and auxiliary) are the middle two letters of your type (your mental function pair, or heart of type). You also have a tertiary and inferior function, which are usually developed later in life.

THE JUNGIAN COMPASS

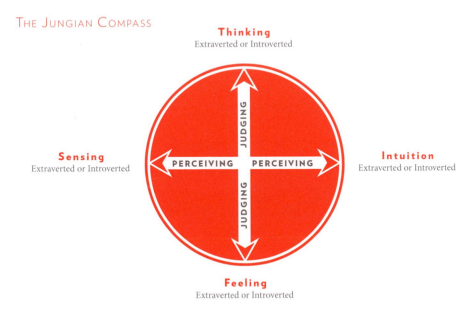

Thinking
Extraverted or Introverted

Sensing
Extraverted or Introverted

Intuition
Extraverted or Introverted

Feeling
Extraverted or Introverted

The Jungian Compass illustrates the concept of type dynamics, an interrelated system of functions working together.

Source: From the **Introduction to Type® Dynamics and Development** booklet by Myers and Kirby. Copyright 1994 by CPP, Inc. All rights reserved.

If you are having trouble determining your type, explore the hierarchy of functions in the table (pp. 76–77) for types you think may be your best fit. Think about whether you use the functions in your outer or inner world. Also, consider the ease with which you make decisions. Decision making is likely easier when using your dominant function, but difficult when using your inferior function. For more information on using personality type in the decision-making process, see CHAPTER 9.

A complete understanding of type dynamics would require much more information. The list of suggested readings at the end of this chapter may provide more information about type dynamics and mental functions. If you take the MBTI instrument, you can also ask your interpreter for additional information about type dynamics.

PERSONALITY PREFERENCES AND CAREER DEVELOPMENT

Personality preferences come into play in a variety of situations, including making career decisions. Because you will spend the majority of your waking hours at work, it is in your best interest to find a work environment that complements your personality preferences. For example, those with a preference for Extraversion may want to spend most of their work hours around people, while those with a preference for Introversion would likely wish to have some time to quietly reflect during the day.

Now that you have identified your best-fit type, you can identify strengths and challenges that may arise throughout your career development process. If you've taken the MBTI instrument, your report may indicate areas of natural ability, as well as challenges. Look over these descriptions and let them inform your decisions.

Operating "Out of Type"

Imagine using out of type behaviors constantly, behaving outside of your natural preferences (like crossing your arms uncomfortably). You would likely be tired and frustrated from always using your non-preferred functions. Using your preferred behaviors and processes requires less effort to produce quality work. However, there is room for *every* type in *every* occupation and career environment. You may just do a particular job in a way that is different and more comfortable for you. Many occupations also require the use of all eight preferences in some way, so being aware of your potential weaknesses is vital. Jake's story provides an example.

The Hierarchy of Functions of Each Type

ISTJ

1. **DOMINANT** introverted Sensing
   Respecting and relying on internally stored data about reality and actual events
2. **AUXILIARY** extraverted Thinking
   Organizing and structuring the external world with logical systems
3. *Tertiary* Feeling
   Considering the impact of decisions on others
4. Inferior extraverted Intuition
   Seeing possibilities and larger connections

ISTP

1. **DOMINANT** introverted Thinking
   Logically organizing vast amounts of specific data about the material world
2. **AUXILIARY** extraverted Sensing
   Focusing on the immediate material realities in the surrounding world
3. *Tertiary* Intuition
   Seeing patterns in daily events
4. Inferior extraverted Feeling
   Factoring in information about people

ESTP

1. **DOMINANT** extraverted Sensing
   Delighting in the endless variety of the world and in spontaneously interacting with it
2. **AUXILIARY** introverted Thinking
   Using logic and expediency to solve practical problems
3. *Tertiary* Feeling
   Noticing how decisions affect people
4. Inferior introverted Intuition
   Forming an internal image of the future

ESTJ

1. **DOMINANT** extraverted Thinking
   Decisively, logically, and efficiently structuring the external environment to achieve specific goals
2. **AUXILIARY** introverted Sensing
   Internally storing specific, realistic data about the material world for quick retrieval
3. *Tertiary* Intuition
   Identifying patterns in data; looking at long-term possibilities
4. Inferior introverted Feeling
   Reviewing decisions in terms of values

ISFJ

1. **DOMINANT** introverted Sensing
   Respecting and relying on internally stored data about people who are important to them
2. **AUXILIARY** extraverted Feeling
   Organizing and structuring the external world to care for people's daily needs
3. *Tertiary* Thinking
   Assessing logical realities
4. Inferior extraverted Intuition
   Recognizing long-term possibilities and connections

ISFP

1. **DOMINANT** introverted Feeling
   Living by strong inner values about honoring people and nature
2. **AUXILIARY** extraverted Sensing
   Focusing on the immediate needs of people in the world around them
3. *Tertiary* Intuition
   Seeing patterns in people's behavior and needs
4. Inferior extraverted Thinking
   Using detached logic to evaluate

ESFP

1. **DOMINANT** extraverted Sensing
   Delighting in the stimulation of interacting with people and embracing the variety of sensing experiences
2. **AUXILIARY** introverted Feeling
   Setting priorities by being attuned to the needs of others
3. *Tertiary* Thinking
   Using logic to assess consequences
4. Inferior introverted Intuition
   Forming insightful internal pictures of people

ESFJ

1. **DOMINANT** extraverted Feeling
   Acting decisively to create an environment that cares for the practical needs of people around them
2. **AUXILIARY** introverted Sensing
   Internally storing specific, detailed information about people
3. *Tertiary* Intuition
   Developing insights into the potential of others
4. Inferior introverted Thinking
   Using detached logic to understand others

THE HIERARCHY OF FUNCTIONS OF EACH TYPE

INFJ

1. **DOMINANT** introverted Intuition
   Becoming centered through insights about people and images of the future

2. **AUXILIARY** extraverted Feeling
   Structuring the external world to support a vision of possibilities for people

3. *Tertiary* Thinking
   Taking account of long-range consequences

4. Inferior extraverted Sensing
   Noticing realistic data about people

INFP

1. **DOMINANT** introverted Feeling
   Filtering everything through a coherent core of personal values based on honoring individuals

2. **AUXILIARY** extraverted Intuition
   Approaching people and ideas with a sense of curiosity and possibility

3. *Tertiary* Sensing
   Focusing on people's daily needs

4. Inferior extraverted Thinking
   Using detachment and logic to evaluate possibilities

ENFP

1. **DOMINANT** extraverted Intuition
   Seeing exciting possibilities for people and enthusiastically pursuing them

2. **AUXILIARY** introverted Feeling
   Evaluating and organizing insights to help people realize their potential

3. *Tertiary* Thinking
   Using detachment and logic to analyze options

4. Inferior introverted Sensing
   Storing and retrieving realistic, practical data

ENFJ

1. **DOMINANT** extraverted Feeling
   Providing the structures and encouragement to energize people and groups to grow

2. **AUXILIARY** introverted Intuition
   Developing innovative ways for people and groups to realize their potential

3. *Tertiary* Sensing
   Considering immediate, practical options

4. Inferior introverted Thinking
   Using detached, precise logic to evaluate interactions

INTJ

1. **DOMINANT** introverted Intuition
   Relying on clear, complex inner pictures of the present and future as a guide

2. **AUXILIARY** extraverted Thinking
   Using logic to express and implement their ideas

3. *Tertiary* Feeling
   Taking account of values

4. Inferior extraverted Sensing
   Factoring in current reality, details

INTP

1. **DOMINANT** introverted Thinking
   Logically organizing information into global systems to understand the world

2. **AUXILIARY** extraverted Intuition
   Approaching ideas and information with curiosity, extrapolating patterns into the future

3. *Tertiary* Sensing
   Giving weight to external realities

4. Inferior extraverted Feeling
   Including the perspectives and needs of people

ENTP

1. **DOMINANT** extraverted Intuition
   Scanning the environment for options, new and stimulating ideas, exciting possibilities

2. **AUXILIARY** introverted Thinking
   Using logic to critique ideas and plan implementation

3. *Tertiary* Feeling
   Factoring in the needs of others

4. Inferior introverted Sensing
   Considering the limitations imposed by reality

ENTJ

1. **DOMINANT** extraverted Thinking
   Directing others decisively, structuring the environment to achieve long-range goals

2. **AUXILIARY** introverted Intuition
   Developing strategies, seeing patterns and possibilities in the present and future

3. *Tertiary* Sensing
   Including details and the steps necessary to achieve goals

4. Inferior introverted Feeling
   Assessing the congruity between values and behaviors

ADAPTATION

Jake (INTP) is a graphic designer at a large advertising agency. He has always had creative energy and loves to come up with new ideas and run with them. This is certainly valued at his company, but upper level management expects deadlines and progress reports throughout each project a designer is working on. Jake would certainly prefer to work creatively without a set deadline, but his occupation requires compromises. Because of this, Jake has practiced operating out of type in the workplace. Although it takes extra effort, he consciously keeps a strict schedule for his work progress. He also has reminders set to update his boss on projects. With an artist's mindset and some extra effort, Jake is able to meet (and exceed) his employer's expectations while producing creative work.

As Jake's situation demonstrates, we live in an environment that doesn't always easily align with each person's natural preferences. Because of this, people must sometimes adapt to environmental expectations. What if you broke your preferred writing hand? You could learn to write legibly with the other hand, but it would take conscious attention and practice to gain the skills.

It's mostly a "J" culture in which we live, work, and go to school, so those with a "P" preference are sometimes forced to adjust. For example, in the professional world, people must keep schedules, meet deadlines, and maintain an organized environment. Many people must also operate out of type during the grade school years, as information is provided nearly always through the senses, making it more comfortable for those with a Sensing preference. Many Intuitive students are not exposed to ways of using their natural Intuitive preference in education until they reach college. Sometimes, our preferences may get in the way of career or academic success, so self-knowledge and willingness to adapt are necessary. Use ACTIVITY 5.1 to reflect on personal experiences of operating out of type.

Type Development

We all have preferences, but we can all operate out of type. How is this so? Over time and experience, we will have opportunities to "exercise" our less preferred functions. Think about a cardio workout. The first time you step on a treadmill, you probably can't run five miles. But with motivation and many workouts, you can build up to it. Type development is much the same. With time and experience, you can strengthen your less preferred functions. This is great news if you have ambitious career dreams that incorporate your least preferred functions!

The timing of developing less preferred functions may vary for each person. Some may have developed their dominant and auxiliary functions by early adulthood, and will develop their tertiary and inferior functions by mid-life. For others, the process may develop more slowly. Life experiences and environments play a role in when and how functions may be fully developed.

CONCLUSION

Personality type is the final element of your Personal Career Profile. Having a complete picture of your personality preferences can lead you to career environments that are likely to be most comfortable for you. Now that you have analyzed your values, skills, interests, and personality, you may be able to see connections and overarching themes among these elements. Next, you will synthesize the elements of your Personal Career Profile, giving you a foundation for researching majors and careers.

CHAPTER 5

ACTIVITIES

ACTIVITY 5.1   **WRITE ABOUT AN OUT-OF-TYPE EXPERIENCE**

Reflect and write about a time when you had to operate outside of one of your preferences. What was this like for you? Next, reflect and write about a time when you operated using a natural preference. Describe the differences between how you operated and felt after the experiences.

SUGGESTED READINGS

- *Do What You Are* by Paul D. Tieger and Barbara Barron-Tieger

- *Gifts Differing* by Isabel B. Myers with Peter B. Myers

- *Introduction to Type* by Isabel Briggs Myers

- *Introduction to Type and Careers* by Allen L. Hammer

- *Introduction to Type Dynamics and Development* by Katharine D. Myers and Linda K. Kirby

- *MBTI Manual* by Isabel Briggs Myers, Mary H. McCaulley, Naomi L. Quenk, and Allen L. Hammer

- *People Types and Tiger Stripes* by Gordon D. Lawrence and Eleanor Sommer

- *Please Understand Me II* by David Keirsey

SUMMARY & KEY POINTS

- People are naturally drawn to work environments and career areas that align with their personality preferences.

- There are four elements of personality: (1) where you focus your energy and attention (Extraversion/Introversion); (2) how you take in information (Sensing/Intuition); (3) how you make decisions (Thinking/Feeling); and (4) how you deal with the outer world (Judging/Perceiving).

- Personality type is not simply a sum of its parts, but rather a dynamic system of interrelationships of the preferences.

- Working in an environment that is out of type for you may require more energy for you to be comfortable and to succeed. However, with practice and experience, you can develop behavior outside of your natural type.

- There is room for *every* type in *every* occupation and career environment, and all eight preferences are used by every person.

MAKE THE CONNECTIONS

"The leg bone connected to the knee bone,
 the knee bone connected to the thigh bone,
 the thigh bone connected to the back bone..."

TRADITIONAL FOLK SONG

As the old song goes, the bones and other parts of your body are connected to each other to shape a whole—your body or "outer self." Similarly, your values (what's important to you), skills (what you do well), interests (what you find enjoyable), and personality (natural preferences), are all related to each other and help to shape your "inner self." To understand your "outer self" you must know how your bones, muscles, and organs work together, and to understand your "inner self" you must know how your values, skills, interests, and personality interrelate.

If you neglect these connections and choose a major that doesn't optimally relate to your whole "inner self," you may end up feeling that your time at college could have been better spent. If you end up in work that doesn't match an important value, or doesn't offer an opportunity to use a favorite skill, or doesn't complement your personality type, or just plain doesn't interest you—or worse, two, three, or all four of these shortcomings—then you could potentially be very unhappy during the majority of your waking hours: at work. But, if you take the time now to do the work of learning as much as you can about yourself, it is much more likely that you will find yourself in a major, and ultimately a career, that will not only be interesting, but deeply rewarding as well.

Learning Objectives

» Appreciate the importance of discovering connections between values, skills, interests, and personality

» Seek out connections between the elements of your Personal Career Profile

» Develop a mission statement to provide direction to your life and work

In deepening your self-awareness, you are following the dictum that has been considered essential to human happiness and wisdom — and pursued by countless men and women — since the time of Ancient Greece: "know thyself."

ACTIVITIES 6.1 through 6.4 will assist you in making connections between the elements of your Personal Career Profile.

CHAPTER 6

ACTIVITIES

Values

List (in rank order) your top five career values. Provide a concrete example (a current or former activity or experience) demonstrating each value (*example:* Flexible Work Schedule: Last Thanksgiving, I didn't let my job keep me from visiting my family over the holidays).

1. _____

_____

_____

2. _____

_____

_____

3. _____

_____

_____

4. _____

_____

_____

5. _____

_____

_____

Skills

List (in rank order) the five skills you most enjoy using, or that you would like to develop. Provide a concrete example (a current or former activity or experience) demonstrating each skill (*example:* Public Speaking: I enjoyed participating on the speech team in high school and gave several successful speeches).

1. _____

_____

_____

2. _____

_____

_____

3. _____

_____

_____

4. _____

_____

_____

5. _____

_____

_____

Interests

List your three-letter "best fit" Holland Theme Code (R = Realistic, I = Investigative, A = Artistic, S = Social, E = Enterprising, C = Conventional).

Your Holland Theme Code

1	2	3

If you've taken the Strong Interest Inventory instrument, look at the Theme Descriptions chart near the top of page 2 of your Strong Interest Inventory profile. Notice that each row of the chart describes one of the six Holland themes. Find your top three themes (as listed in the box above), and for each theme, look at the "Interests" and "Work Activities" columns. For each theme, select three to five words or phrases that best describe your interests from these two boxes and write them down on the next page. Provide a concrete, personal example (a former or current activity or experience) that demonstrates each theme. (If you haven't taken the Strong Interest Inventory instrument, review the Holland interest themes in CHAPTER 4 [pp. 50–55], and use phrases that best describe you for each of the three themes in your "best fit" Holland Theme Code above.)

EXAMPLE:

Theme: Investigative
Research, performing lab work, solving abstract problems

Example: I did an independent research project in my high school chemistry lab and really enjoyed it.

Theme: _____
Words or Phrases that Describe My Interests:

_____

Example:

_____

_____

Theme: _____
Words or Phrases that Describe My Interests:

_____

Example:

_____

_____

Theme: _____
Words or Phrases that Describe My Interests:

_____

Example:

_____

_____

MAKE THE CONNECTIONS **89**

From the multiple lists of words or phrases that describe your interests, copy (in rank order) your top five words or phrases below.

1. _____

2. _____

3. _____

4. _____

5. _____

Personality

If you've taken the Myers-Briggs Type Indicator instrument, circle your four MBTI preferences ("best fit" type) and provide a brief definition of each preference using the top of page 3 of your MBTI Career Report and/or the descriptions in CHAPTER 5 [pp. 66–69]. Provide a concrete, personal example (a current or former activity or experience) that demonstrates each preference. (If you haven't taken the MBTI instrument, review the descriptions of the four dichotomies in CHAPTER 5 [pp. 66–69], self-select your preference for each dichotomy, and define each preference by using relevant phrases. Then provide a concrete, personal example as discussed above.)

Circle one: **Extraversion** or **Introversion**

Brief Definition:

_____

_____

Example:

_____

_____

Circle one: **Sensing** or **Intuition**

Brief Definition:

_____

Example:

_____

_____

Circle one: **Thinking** or **Feeling**

Brief Definition:

_____

Example:

_____

_____

Circle one: **Judging** or **Perceiving**

Brief Definition:

_____

Example:

_____

_____

Next, review your MBTI profile (or if you haven't taken the MBTI instrument, the description of your self-estimated type in the Type Table on pp. 72–73). Choose five words or brief phrases from the description of your type that match you best, and write them below (you may shorten phrases to a few essential words).

1. _____

2. _____

3. _____

4. _____

5. _____

ACTIVITY 6.2 **MAKE CONNECTIONS**

In this activity, you will take the descriptive words or phrases you wrote in ACTIVITY 6.1 and look for connections between them.

Begin by taking each one of your top five values (as listed in ACTIVITY 6.1) and compare it to your list of top five skills (as listed in ACTIVITY 6.1). Look for meaningful connections.

Write down connections you find between each listed value and your top five skills, and write a brief explanation of the connection. Then, do the same for values and interests, values and personality, and so on. What are all the possible connections you can find? Complete the following six tables, connecting the elements you listed in ACTIVITY 6.1.

Note that:

- You may find multiple connections for a single term; conversely, there may be terms you do not find any connections for.

- You don't need to complete all three rows of each box (though you should try).

- You don't need to write your connections in any particular order.

Value	Skill	Connection
Example: Creativity	Present	Presenting can be highly creative.
Example: Pay & Profit	Sell	Salespeople can make great money.

Value	Interest	Connection

Value	Personality	Connection

Skill	Interest	Connection

Skill	Personality	Connection

Interest	Personality	Connection

Look over the connections you discovered. Now, look for connections between the connections. How many matches can you find between all four parts of your Personal Career Profile?

Value	Skill	Interest	Personality	Connection
Example: People	Listening	Helping	Caring Environment	Serving People's Spiritual Needs

Which of the above connections is most clear, meaningful, or exciting to you?

If Finding Connections Is Challenging...

There are several reasons that it can be challenging to make connections between all four parts of your Personal Career Profile:

- You may have looked at it too much. (Take a break and review it again later.)

- You may be assuming that you've already found all the possible connections. (Almost everyone can find additional connections if they look carefully.)

- There may be incongruities between parts of your Personal Career Profile. (Look for connections between two or three parts, instead of all four.)

- You are unsure what certain terms mean, such as specific skills or interest themes. (Review the relevant chapters to improve your understanding.)

CONNECTIONS IN CONFLICT

What if some aspects of your Personal Career Profile appear to *conflict* more than they *connect*? After assessing their values, skills, interests, and personality, Toby and Adam both discovered that they valued high pay, but that they were also interested in the clinical helping professions, which they perceived as having low pay.

Toby, who loves studying, learned that by obtaining a graduate or professional degree she could earn a Ph.D. in psychology or an M.D. in psychiatry, and that either degree would allow her to satisfy both her value of making good money and her interest in helping others.

(continued)

CONNECTIONS IN CONFLICT *(continued)*

Adam, however, wasn't interested in the many years of additional schooling that Toby's plan would require. Some creative brainstorming helped him realize that there were other options. He could aim toward a higher-paying profession such as pharmaceutical sales while doing people-oriented volunteer work in his free time, or aim toward a lower-paying helping profession position and begin a part-time Internet business on the side to make extra money. Either way, like Toby, Adam would be able to satisfy both his value and interest.

If parts of *you* seem to be in conflict, take some time to research and brainstorm as many possibilities as you can. Like Toby, you may discover other options that will resolve the apparent discord. Or like Adam, you may find a creative way to resolve the impasse.

ACTIVITY 6.3 **IMAGINE A DREAM CAREER**

Look at the "connections between the connections" you discovered at the end of ACTIVITY 6.2. Take one connection you found between all four parts of your Personal Career Profile, and imagine what such a job would look like. If you know about an existing career that you believe fits all four, write about that. But if you don't, create your own description of a career that includes all four components. Don't worry if you're not sure this occupation exists—you may find it through research, or you may invent a brand new career!

ACTIVITY 6.4   **CREATE YOUR MISSION STATEMENT FOR WORK AND LIFE**

A mission statement provides direction for your life's work. It's like a blueprint, personal credo, or motto that states what your life is about.

From the lists below select words according to the instructions. These will be the raw materials for your mission statement. In each of the four steps feel free to add words not listed.

Step One: Action Verbs

Every mission requires action, and action words are verbs. Circle verbs from the list below that are the most meaningful, purposeful, exciting, or inspiring to you.

- Achieve
- Adapt
- Analyze
- Arrange
- Believe
- Collect
- Command
- Communicate
- Commit
- Compete
- Connect
- Create

- Decide
- Develop
- Discuss
- Excite
- Facilitate
- Focus
- Harmonize
- Imagine
- Include
- Initiate
- Inspire
- Learn

- Manage
- Organize
- Recognize
- Relate
- Remember
- Resolve
- Respect
- Transform
- Understand
- Welcome

Narrow to just three choices below and add any verbs you like which might not be on the list.

A	**B**	**C**

Step Two: Universal Values and Principles

What universal value, principle, or purpose would you be willing to devote your life to, or defend to the death? What is your essence? Circle all that interest you below.

- Awareness
- Balance
- Beauty
- Benevolence
- Bliss
- Caring
- Change
- Charity
- Comfort
- Community
- Compassion
- Connection
- Consciousness
- Cooperation
- Courage
- Creativity
- Devotion
- Dignity
- Equality
- Excellence
- Excitement
- Faith
- Fellowship
- Forgiveness
- Freedom
- Generosity

- Gentleness
- Goodness
- Grace
- Gratitude
- Harmony
- Health
- Honesty
- Honor
- Hope
- Hospitality
- Humility
- Humor
- Initiative
- Inner Peace
- Integrity
- Joy
- Justice
- Kindness
- Learning
- Life
- Love
- Loyalty
- Mercy
- Nature
- Order
- Patience

- Peace
- Perseverance
- Positive attitude
- Power
- Purity
- Relationships
- Reliability
- Respect
- Responsibility
- Sacrifice
- Safety
- Self-expression
- Self-sufficiency
- Self-worth
- Service
- Simplicity
- Solitude
- Tranquility
- Trust
- Truth
- Understanding
- Unity
- Vitality
- Wholeness
- Wisdom

Narrow your choice to one and write it below.

D

Step Three: Passions

Read the following list of causes, issues, and fields. Most of the specific causes below likely have two or more sides to them (e.g., "Drug laws"), and the larger fields may have multiple issue areas within them (e.g., "Democracy"). Circle all that interest you.

- Abortion
- Administration
- Affirmative action
- Agriculture
- AIDS
- Alcoholism
- Animal rights/welfare
- Art
- Art funding
- Bioethics
- Books
- Border issues
- Broadcasting
- Campaign finance reform
- Cancer
- Child abuse/neglect
- Childcare
- Children's rights/Child labor
- Civil liberties
- Civil rights
- Clean/Renewable energy
- Cloning
- Community-building
- Construction
- Consumerism
- Corporate power
- Crime
- Criminal laws
- Death penalty
- Defense

- Deforestation
- Democracy
- Design
- Disarmament
- Domestic violence
- Drug abuse
- Drug laws
- Economic justice
- Education
- Eldercare
- Entertainment
- Environmental justice
- Equality
- Euthanasia
- Extinction of species
- Family issues
- Farming/Gardening
- Fashion
- Fathers' rights
- Finance
- Food
- Free speech
- Freedom of the press
- Gambling
- Gangs
- Genocide
- GLBT rights
- Global warming
- Globalization
- Government

- Growth and sprawl
- Gun rights/Gun control
- Hate crimes
- Health and healthcare
- Homelessness
- Housing
- Human development
- Hunger
- Immigration
- Information technology
- Insurance
- Journalism
- Justice system
- Labor
- Landmines
- Law
- Literacy
- Management
- Media
- Mental health (depression and anxiety)
- Military-industrial complex/Arms trade
- Military spending
- Music
- National debt
- Natural disasters
- News
- Organic food
- Overpopulation

(continued)

- Parks and recreation
- Peace/War issues
- People with disabilities
- Police officer misconduct
- Police officer rights
- Political prisoners
- Politics
- Pollution and hazardous waste
- Pornography
- Poverty
- Prison industry
- Prisoners' rights
- Proliferation of WMDs
- Prostitution
- Public safety
- Publicity
- Publishing
- Racism
- Real estate
- Refugees
- Religion
- Religious freedom
- Reproductive issues
- School performance
- School violence
- Separation of church and state
- Sex education
- Sexual assault
- Size of government
- Slavery and human trafficking
- Smoking and tobacco industry
- Social justice
- Societal apathy and despair
- Space exploration
- Spirituality
- Sports
- Suicide
- Taxation
- Technology
- Terrorism
- Tourism
- Transportation
- Unemployment
- Urban planning
- Veterans' rights
- Victims' rights
- Waste and recycling
- Wealth disparities
- Welfare
- Women's rights
- Workplace discrimination

Narrow your choices to two and write them below.

E   F

Step Four: Service

Circle any words of interest based on what people, groups, and/or organizations you feel drawn to serve, be around, inspire, learn from, or impact. As with the above lists, feel free to use other people, groups, or organizations not on this list.

Organizations and Needs	Populations

Organizations and Needs

- Education
- Environment
- Finance
- Government
- Healthcare
- Housing
- International
- Legal advice
- Local organizations
- National
- Nonprofit
- Parenting concerns
- Private sector/Business
- Religious organizations
- Research
- State
- Universities

Populations

- Animals
- At risk students
- Children
- College
- Disabled
- Ethnic minorities
- Hospitalized
- International students
- Men
- Parents
- Peers (your age)
- Poor/Homeless
- Professionals
- Refugees
- Senior citizens
- Singles
- Teens
- Women
- Young adults

Narrow your choices to two and write them below.

G   H

Step Five: Constructing your Mission Statement

Using the words you placed on lines A through H on the previous pages, complete this formula:

My mission is to:

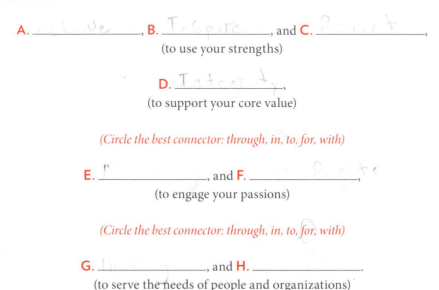

A. _____ Ve _____, B. _____ Inspire _____, and C. _____ Respect _____,

(to use your strengths)

D. _____ Integrity _____,

(to support your core value)

(Circle the best connector: through, in, to, for, with)

E. _____ I _____, and F. _____ Respects _____,

(to engage your passions)

(Circle the best connector: through, in, to, for, with)

G. _____ _____, and H. _____.

(to serve the needs of people and organizations)

Your mission statement:

_____

_____

_____

_____

Step Six: Clarifying Your Mission Statement

Simplify your mission statement by removing words that are not essential; change word order to make your focus clearer.

_____

_____

_____

_____

This Mission Statement activity is adapted from an activity created by Joan Pedersen, Ph.D. (unpublished).

CHAPTER 6

SUMMARY & KEY POINTS

- Understanding the connections between your values, skills, interests, and personality will help you choose a major and career path that are optimal for you.

- By considering your universal values, passions, and those whom you would like to serve, your mission becomes your means for fulfilling your life's purpose.

EXPLORING AND CHOOSING MAJORS

"An investment in knowledge always pays the best interest."

BENJAMIN FRANKLIN, AMERICAN STATESMAN

INTRODUCTION

At some point, you've undoubtedly been asked the question, "What is your major?" (If you haven't, rest assured, this question is coming.) Maybe you had an easy time answering, maybe not. Choosing a major can seem like a scary and sometimes overwhelming proposition, but it doesn't have to be. While there is no magic formula for choosing a major, proper reflection and research will equip you to make an informed decision.

YOUR PERSONAL CAREER PROFILE IN MAJOR RESEARCH

Perhaps one of the most challenging aspects of researching potential majors is figuring out which majors you'd like to learn more about, as there are many to choose from. In CHAPTERS 2–6, you learned about your values, skills, interests, and personality and made connections between them. Ideally, your Personal Career Profile will serve as a starting point for determining which majors to research and will ultimately help you choose a major that you enjoy.

Learning Objectives

» Recognize that academic institutions are structured differently and understand how yours is organized

» Learn how to identify the various degrees and certifications available at your college or university

» Understand the complex relationship between majors and careers

NUTS AND BOLTS: HOW ACADEMIC INSTITUTIONS ARE ORGANIZED

The first hurdle to overcome when choosing an academic program is understanding the organization of your institution, which is often very complex. Right now, your job is to gather information about academic programs that are of interest to you. In order to efficiently gather the best information possible, it is important to understand how majors and other programs of study are organized at your institution.

Universities, Colleges, Schools, and Departments

While there is no "cookie-cutter" model, generally, a large university is divided into several separate schools (sometimes called colleges). For example, a large university may be divided into the following schools and colleges:

- College of Arts and Sciences
- School of Agriculture
- School of Business
- School of Continuing Studies
- School of Dentistry
- School of Education
- School of Engineering and Technology
- School of Journalism
- School of Library and Information Sciences

- School of Medicine
- School of Music
- School of Nursing
- School of Optometry
- School of Public and Environmental Affairs
- School of Public Health
- School of Social Work

Each of these schools or colleges is further divided into departments. For example, a College of Arts and Sciences (a liberal arts school) may be broken up into many departments, such as Biology, Criminal Justice, English, History, Mathematics, Psychology, and Telecommunications, to name a few. A School of Business may consist of Accounting, Finance, Management, and Marketing departments. A School of Education may be divided into different departments for Early Childhood Education, Elementary Education, and Secondary Education. Keep in mind that none of these lists are exhaustive and how departments are divided and subdivided may vary greatly from one institution to another.

SAMPLE ACADEMIC STRUCTURE

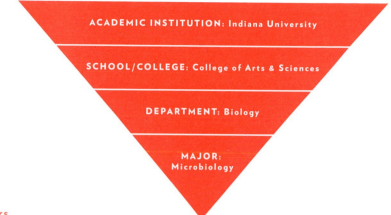

ACADEMIC INSTITUTION: Indiana University

SCHOOL/COLLEGE: College of Arts & Sciences

DEPARTMENT: Biology

MAJOR: Microbiology

Majors

A major is a field of study that you specialize in that may or may not have a direct correlation to your future career (we'll discuss the relationship of major to career later). A major will be found within a specific department of a school or college. For example, a Spanish major might be included in the Foreign Language Department that is within the College of Arts and Sciences. While it's almost impossible to make a blanket statement about major requirements, there are some generalities worth mentioning. Often, the number of classes taken within your major will account for approximately one-third of your total classes. However, there are some areas of study, such as business and education, with more courses required for the major. These will be your most specialized and potentially most advanced classes, focusing on your chosen field of study.

SAMPLE DEGREE REQUIREMENTS

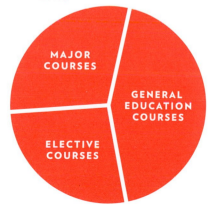

MAJOR COURSES

GENERAL EDUCATION COURSES

ELECTIVE COURSES

When considering majors, you might also think about the possibility of a *double major*, in which a student has two majors. These majors may or may not be within the same school or department, but they will both result in the same type of degree (for example, both majors may result in a Bachelor of Science). It is important to note that a double major is different from a *dual degree*, in which a student pursues two separate degrees (for example, a Bachelor of Science and a Bachelor of Arts). Whether or not a double major or dual degree is right for you depends on your academic and career goals as well as the potential workload it might entail. If you are considering a double major or dual degree, discuss these factors with an academic advisor.

CREATING AN INDIVIDUALIZED MAJOR

An "individualized" (or "specialized") major is an option that allows you to combine different courses into a major that doesn't already exist. Such a major is an excellent option for students whose specific interests and needs are not met by any of the available majors or "tracks" at their institution. For example, Will Shortz, a student at Indiana University, was interested in the study of puzzles, even though there was no such major. Fortunately, Indiana had an individualized major program that allowed him to create a major in enigmatology, the study of puzzle construction. Will received his degree in enigmatology and, in time, went on to become the Crossword Puzzles Editor for the New York Times. While this option may not be available at every institution and the approval process may be quite lengthy, it may be worth looking into.

For those who have a specific interest but do not want to or are unable to pursue a major in that area, there are numerous options, including minors, certificates, and concentrations.

Minors

A minor is an academic subject requiring fewer courses than a major and allows you to broaden your knowledge while also exposing you to advanced concepts. A minor may require only a few classes, depending on your academic institution.

Certification and Concentration Programs

Another route toward strengthening your degree and broadening your knowledge in an interest area is a certificate or concentration program. Often, the amount of coursework in such a program may be similar to that of a minor and may fulfill a requirement for licensure in a given profession.

While minors, certifications, and concentrations are usually not required, they are beneficial in that they allow you to study in various academic fields and lead to a more well-rounded academic experience. Furthermore, this increased exposure may even help expand your career opportunities.

RYAN'S "MAJOR" DILEMMA

Ryan, like many college students, was unsure of what he wanted to major in. He had many interests, including history and Spanish, but also felt that it could be helpful to study business. Upon much self-reflection as well as numerous meetings with his academic and career advisors, Ryan realized that his passion was history and decided to major in it. While relieved to have his major figured out, he still wanted to pursue Spanish in some capacity and at least gain some exposure to general business courses. Ryan figured out that he could minor in Spanish, add a business certificate, and still graduate on time. In the end, Ryan was able to study the three areas he enjoyed most, gaining a breadth of knowledge and diverse set of skills.

WHAT MAJORS ARE OUT THERE?

At this point, you may be wondering how to discover what areas of study exist. Perhaps the most exhaustive list available is the *Classification of Instructional Programs (CIP)*. The CIP is used by the U.S. Department of Education to track, assess, and report fields of study at institutions of higher education throughout the United States. While the CIP likely lists more offerings than are available at your school, it is interesting to note all of the options. If you find something of interest that is not available at your school, the individualized major previously discussed could be an option. In some cases, you may even wish to consider another academic institution if your field of interest is not offered. Before you make any significant decisions, make sure you discuss all of your options with an academic advisor. See ACTIVITY 7.1 to explore many of the areas of study included on the CIP.

RESEARCHING MAJORS AND OTHER ACADEMIC PROGRAMS

Now that you've had the chance to look at the possible areas of study, you'll want to start narrowing down your list and more thoroughly researching areas that are of particular interest to you. The following strategies will be useful.

School Websites, Course Catalogs, and Academic Bulletins

As we've already established, it's important to be familiar with the structure of your particular academic institution, as well as what majors are actually offered and what they entail. School websites (institution-wide or school- or department-specific), course catalogs, and academic bulletins provide the most up-to-date, accurate information about areas of study at your institution.

People

As a college student, your access to those who are experts in their field of study is greater than it will ever be. If you're considering a certain major, who better to talk to than faculty and advisors in that field? For a different perspective, talking to current students and alumni of that major can be helpful also. If you are interested in connecting with such students or alumni, a faculty member or academic advisor may be able to steer you in the right direction. The following list of questions may help guide your conversations:

- What career fields have graduates of this major pursued?
- What specific organizations have hired graduates of this major and what have their career paths looked like?
- What are the prerequisites for admission to this school/college, department, or major?
- Is there a minimum GPA requirement?
- What is the admission process?
- What courses and experiences are required to complete this major?
- What type(s) of experiential requirements (externship, internship, practicum) are there?
- Will any of the courses I have already taken apply toward this major?
- What further coursework will be required?

- What skill set(s) will I develop through this major?
- What are some downfalls/disadvantages of this major? What might I dislike?

Based on your findings, does this seem like a good fit with your own needs and goals?

Classes

Another way to see if a particular field of study or major is a good fit for you is by taking classes. By taking one or more 100–200 level courses, you should get an overview of what classes in the major are like, and you'll have a chance to meet faculty and students already in the discipline. Even if you decide not to continue on with the major, the class may count toward a minor, certificate, general education, or elective requirement. If you are unable to take any courses, reviewing the syllabi and textbooks for specific courses (which most academic departments have readily available), can also provide useful insights.

Online Resources

Of the many resources that are available online, two are especially helpful. The U.S. Department of Labor's *O*NET Resource Center* website and the electronic version of the *Occupational Outlook Handbook* include educational requirements and detailed information about hundreds of occupations. These resources and the types of information that can be found in them will be discussed in greater detail in CHAPTER 8.

RELATIONSHIP BETWEEN MAJOR AND CAREER

As you go about exploring and choosing a major, are you worried that you might choose something that doesn't have a direct path to a career? Are you worried that you will waste your time in a major that you will end up not using? Are you tempted to choose a "safe major" that has a clear career direction after graduation? If you answered "yes" to any of these questions, you are not alone.

Changing Majors

» The tools and strategies discussed in this chapter will help you choose a major that meets your needs and that you enjoy. However, you may choose a major that does not end up being a good fit and decide that a change is in your best interest. Changing majors is common and should not be viewed as negative. While you do not want to make a habit out of changing your major, it is both important and reassuring to recognize it as an option.

In fact, career advisors hear these concerns every day. Rest assured, there is value in majors that directly relate to a career as well as those that do not.

Direct Relationship

A major with a direct relationship has an obvious path toward a specific career. Often, such a job or career requires training, licensure, or certification that needs to be acquired as part of your academic program or soon after. Two examples are an accounting major who becomes an accountant, or an education major who becomes a teacher. But just because a major may have a direct relationship to a certain career, doesn't mean that one has to go in that career direction. For example, an accounting major may decide to pursue a career as a real estate agent, something completely unrelated to accounting.

Indirect Relationship

While it would be convenient if all majors aligned so nicely to potential careers as the examples given previously, the reality is that many do not. Those majors that do not have this clear path have an indirect relationship to potential careers. This can be both frustrating and exciting at the same time. Your values, skills, interests, and personality, combined with experiences outside of the classroom that you may have had, can help guide you to a career that may not have anything to do with your major. With relevant experiences or advanced degrees, an English major could pursue a career as an advertising executive, a healthcare professional, or a counselor, to name a few options. See ACTIVITY 7.3 to explore how some of the majors that you may be considering connect to careers.

CONCLUSION

In this chapter, we have discussed how academic institutions are organized, how to research programs of study, and the relationships between majors and careers. Deciding on a major is usually not something that happens overnight. You should allow yourself time to use the tools that we have discussed, and realize that there may be times when you will get frustrated. Finally, while this is a "major" decision, it does not have to dictate your career choice and is only one of many factors that will influence your choice of work.

CHAPTER 7

ACTIVITIES

ACTIVITY 7.1 **EXPLORE MAJORS**

The following list contains a sampling of the more common areas of study that you may find at many institutions. As you go through the list, check off those majors that sound interesting. If you're unsure about what a particular major is, but feel that it piques your interest in some way, check it.

☐ Accounting

☐ Adult and Continuing Education

☐ Advertising

☐ Aerospace Science

☐ African American Studies

☐ African Studies/Language

☐ Agriculture

☐ American Studies

☐ Anatomy

☐ Animal Science

☐ Anthropology

☐ Apparel and Textiles

☐ Arabic

☐ Archeology

☐ Architecture

☐ Art

☐ Arts Management

☐ Asian Studies/Language

☐ Astronomy/Astrophysics

☐ Athletic Training

☐ Audiology and Hearing Sciences

☐ Biochemistry

☐ Biology

☐ Biotechnology

☐ Botany

☐ Business

☐ Ceramics

☐ Chemistry

☐ Child Development

☐ Classical Civilization

☐ Clinical Laboratory Science

☐ Cognitive Science

☐ Communication and Culture

☐ Comparative Arts

☐ Comparative Literature

☐ Computer Science and Information Technology

☐ Creative Writing

☐ Criminal Justice

☐ Cytotechnology

☐ Dance

☐ Dental Hygiene

☐ Dietetics

☐ Dutch Studies

☐ East Asian Language and Cultures

☐ East Asian Studies

☐ Economics

☐ Education

☐ Engineering

☐ English

☐ Entrepreneurship

☐ Environmental Management

☐ Environmental Science

☐ Entomology

☐ European Studies

- ☐ Exercise Science
- ☐ Fashion Design
- ☐ Finance
- ☐ Fitness Specialist
- ☐ Folklore
- ☐ French
- ☐ Game Studies
- ☐ Gender Studies
- ☐ General Studies
- ☐ Geography
- ☐ Geological Sciences
- ☐ German
- ☐ Government
- ☐ Graphic Design
- ☐ Greek
- ☐ Health Administration
- ☐ Health, Physical Education, and Recreation
- ☐ Hebrew
- ☐ History
- ☐ Human Biology
- ☐ Human Development/Family Studies
- ☐ Human Resources
- ☐ Human Sexuality
- ☐ India Studies
- ☐ Industrial Design
- ☐ Informatics
- ☐ Interior Design

- ☐ International Studies
- ☐ Islamic Studies
- ☐ Italian
- ☐ Japanese
- ☐ Jewish Studies
- ☐ Journalism (Print)
- ☐ Journalism (Broadcast)
- ☐ Kinesiology
- ☐ Korean
- ☐ Labor Studies
- ☐ Latin
- ☐ Latin American and Caribbean Studies
- ☐ Latino Studies
- ☐ Legal Studies
- ☐ Linguistics
- ☐ Management
- ☐ Marine Biology
- ☐ Marketing
- ☐ Mathematics
- ☐ Medical Imaging Technology
- ☐ Medieval Studies
- ☐ Microbiology
- ☐ Middle/Near Eastern Studies
- ☐ Music
- ☐ Near Eastern Languages and Cultures

- ☐ Neuroscience
- ☐ Nuclear Medicine Technology
- ☐ Nursing
- ☐ Nutrition Science
- ☐ Oceanography
- ☐ Operations Management
- ☐ Optometric Technology
- ☐ Outdoor Recreation and Resource Management
- ☐ Paleontology
- ☐ Paramedic Science
- ☐ Park and Recreation Management
- ☐ Pharmacy
- ☐ Philosophy
- ☐ Photography
- ☐ Physics
- ☐ Policy Studies
- ☐ Political Science
- ☐ Portuguese
- ☐ Pre-Occupational Therapy Study
- ☐ Pre-Physical Therapy Study
- ☐ Pre-Physician Assistant Study
- ☐ Predental Study
- ☐ Prelaw Study
- ☐ Premedical Study

- ☐ Preoptometry Study
- ☐ Prepharmacy Study
- ☐ Preveterinary Study
- ☐ Psychology
- ☐ Public and Environmental Affairs
- ☐ Public and Nonprofit Management
- ☐ Public Financial Management
- ☐ Public Health
- ☐ Public Policy
- ☐ Radiation Therapy
- ☐ Radiography
- ☐ Recording Arts
- ☐ Recreational Sport Management
- ☐ Religious Studies
- ☐ Respiratory Therapy
- ☐ Safety Science
- ☐ Slavic Studies
- ☐ Social Work
- ☐ Sociology
- ☐ South Asian Studies
- ☐ Southeast Asian Studies
- ☐ Spanish
- ☐ Speech and Hearing Sciences
- ☐ Sport Communication Broadcast and Print
- ☐ Sport Marketing and Management
- ☐ Statistics
- ☐ Studio Art
- ☐ Supply Chain Management
- ☐ Telecommunications
- ☐ Theatre and Drama
- ☐ Therapeutic Recreation
- ☐ Tourism Management
- ☐ Urban Studies
- ☐ Women's Studies
- ☐ West European Studies
- ☐ Yiddish Studies
- ☐ Zoology

ACTIVITY 7.2 **MAJORS AT YOUR INSTITUTION**

Using college/university publications, websites, course catalogs, and academic bulletins, find a complete list of the majors that are available at your institution. How does the list compare to that used in ACTIVITY 7.1? Are there any areas of study that show up on the list from ACTIVITY 7.1 that don't show up on your institution's list? If so, you may want to discuss your options with an academic or career advisor.

ACTIVITY 7.3 **CAREERS YOU MIGHT PURSUE**

Based on your findings from ACTIVITIES 7.1 and 7.2, choose three to five majors that you find especially interesting. Using the resources in this chapter, brainstorm careers that are commonly associated with these majors.

CHAPTER 7

SUMMARY & KEY POINTS

- Academic institutions are structured differently, and the first step in researching potential fields of study is understanding how yours is organized.

- Once you understand how your academic institution is organized, it is important to recognize what degrees, majors, minors and certifications are available and how to learn more about them.

- Your major may have a direct or indirect relationship to potential careers and while very important, it is just one of many factors that will shape your career.

DISCOVERING YOUR CAREER OPTIONS

"Your work is to discover your work and then with all your heart to give yourself to it."

BUDDHA, SPIRITUAL TEACHER

INTRODUCTION

Now that you know how to explore majors and understand their relationship to potential careers, this chapter will take your exploration a step further and discuss how to research careers. Career research is especially important because many college students have limited knowledge of what careers actually exist. Much like researching majors, this type of research can seem like an overwhelming undertaking if you don't know where to start. This chapter will advise you on the types of information to look for, how to look for it, and where to gain valuable exposure to career options—all while considering your values, skills, interests, and personality—in order to evaluate careers that may be a good fit for you.

YOUR PERSONAL CAREER PROFILE AND CAREER RESEARCH

As with researching majors, a challenging aspect of researching potential careers is figuring out which ones you'd like to learn more about. As with major research, your Personal Career Profile will serve as a starting point for determining which careers to explore. If you are having trouble identifying careers that you'd like to learn more about, taking assessments such as those that we have already discussed may be very helpful.

Learning Objectives

» Recognize how your values, skills, interests, and personality relate to careers

» Identify the types of information to evaluate when conducting career research

» Understand the various resources, both broad and field-specific, for conducting effective research

» Realize the importance of experiential learning in the career research process

Information to Look for When Researching Careers

» Daily activities

» Working conditions

» Location

» Required education and training

» Desired personal characteristics

The two main assessments that have been discussed in this text are the Strong Interest Inventory®(SII) instrument and the Myers-Briggs Type Indicator®(MBTI) instrument. From a career standpoint, your interests are a strong factor when considering career choice, while your personality is a strong factor when considering career fit. For those who have taken them, these assessments provide occupational scales (SII instrument) and job families (MBTI instrument) that serve as an excellent starting point for deciding which careers to research. It is, however, important to keep in mind that these lists merely serve as suggestions, not "prescriptions." Conversely, if there are careers not listed on your assessment reports that you are interested in researching, you should definitely do so.

CAREER RESEARCH RESOURCES

With all of the information that is available, knowing where to start and what resources to use can be intimidating. This section will introduce some of the most common and useful resources available, while recommending strategies and techniques to tailor your specific search.

Occupational Outlook Handbook

The *Occupational Outlook Handbook (OOH)* is a publication that is released by the U.S. Department of Labor every two years and is available in hard-copy form as well as online. The OOH lists hundreds of jobs and discusses useful information such as:

- Training and education needed

- Earnings

- Projected growth

- What workers do on the job

- Working conditions

O*NET (Occupational Information Network)

The U.S. Department of Labor's *Occupational Information Network* (O*NET) serves as the nation's primary source of occupational information, providing comprehensive information about key attributes and characteristics of workers and occupations. The database is provided online at no cost, and is one of the most up-to-date resources available.

Vocational Biographies

Vocational Biographies is a compilation of over a thousand career profiles of people in many popular occupations, and is available both online and in hard copy. Among many of the subjects discussed by the interviewees are likes and dislikes about their jobs, their career paths, typical responsibilities and activities, training, qualifications, and salary.

Career Exploration Books

There are countless books available that explore almost any career you can think of. These books are often field- or career-specific and go into far greater detail than the resources we have already discussed. For example, a person interested in pursuing a career in education might refer to the book *Opportunities in Teaching Careers*. Likewise, a political science major trying to figure out what she can do with her degree might check out the book *Great Jobs for Political Science Majors*.

Professional Associations

Joining a professional association for a field that you are interested in can be an invaluable source of career information. Professional associations (such as the American Marketing Association) exist to give people working in a field the opportunity to connect with one another as well as to provide training and development for their members. Such associations may be found at the state, regional, and national levels and can provide you with an excellent chance to network with and learn from professionals already in the field. Many professional associations offer discounted student memberships.

For more information about any of the resources discussed in this chapter (and many that are not), visit your campus career center. See ACTIVITY 8.1 to begin identifying and researching careers using the resources we have discussed thus far.

CAREER RESEARCH THROUGH EXPERIENTIAL LEARNING

There are only so many questions you can answer through reading books, journals, and websites. Gaining firsthand knowledge and insight into what a job or career field actually entails can be invaluable. While all of the resources we have already discussed are very useful, they are mostly objective in nature and do not provide the personal, subjective perspective that hands-on experience can. Experiential learning (learning by doing) is an excellent tool for researching both majors and careers. While there are many ways to gain experience, the six best types of experiential learning are informational interviewing, job shadowing, externships, part-time jobs, volunteering, and internships.

Informational Interviewing

The purpose of an informational interview is to acquire information from a person whose career path you are interested in learning more about. As opposed to a job interview, *you* will be the one asking the questions and leading the discussion.

The first goal of an informational interview is to get answers to questions and gain insight into what a certain job or career entails. In this setting, you will learn about aspects of the job, both good and bad, that may not have occurred to you previously. Furthermore, a current employee is best qualified to answer organization-specific questions that you may have.

Equally important is the opportunity to network and expand your list of contacts. You may have heard the phrase, "it's what you know and who you know." This statement is certainly true when it comes to finding a job and is the second benefit of informational interviewing. While talking to people you don't know may seem uncomfortable at first, it will serve you well in the long run. In the interview, you may find out information about current or future employment opportunities. In taking the time and initiative to conduct an informational interview, you will have demonstrated a genuine interest to the interviewer and may remain on her "radar" as a potential candidate.

To identify someone to interview, ask friends, relatives, or any other members of your network for suggestions. You can also contact faculty members, academic advisors, or your campus career center. Another useful resource is your school's alumni office, which may have names and contact information of former students who are working in career fields that interest you.

To arrange an informational interview, consider emailing to request a phone or in-person appointment. In your message, introduce yourself and explain how you received the person's contact information, what you hope to gain from the interview, and the tangible steps for scheduling the appointment.

SAMPLE QUESTIONS FOR AN INFORMATIONAL INTERVIEW

Occupational Requirements and Experience

- How did you get started in this field? Is that typical of most people?
- Describe a typical day and/or week. Would these duties be the same for anyone with your job title?
- What skills and personal qualities are most important for success in this job?

Occupational Environment

- How would you describe the professional climate in your office? In your industry?
- What portions of your job involve interaction with coworkers, clients, or vendors?
- How much evening, weekend, or overtime work is required? What about traveling?

Benefits and Challenges

- What are the greatest rewards of your work?
- What are the greatest frustrations? How do you deal with them?
- On what basis are professionals in your field evaluated? How is success measured?
- What is the starting salary range for new professionals in this field? (Do not ask the person about her specific salary.)

Occupational Outlook

- What are the opportunities for advancement in this field? Could you describe a typical promotional path?

(continued)

SAMPLE QUESTIONS FOR AN INFORMATIONAL INTERVIEW *(continued)*

- What are some growth areas in this field and what impact is that growth likely to have on job opportunities?
- How is the field likely to be affected by changes in technology?

Advice

- What kinds of education or specialized training would best prepare me to do this kind of work?
- What classes can I take, or projects can I complete, that will also be helpful?
- Are there any professional organizations that would help me build my network in this field?
- How do people find out about job openings in your line of work?
- Where do people in this field typically look for internship and job opportunities?
- Who makes the decision to hire someone for this kind of job?

Job Shadowing

Job shadowing is a way to glimpse into an actual "day in the life" of a job or career field. A job-shadowing experience gives you the chance to follow someone around at work for anywhere from a few hours to a few days. You will see the type of environment the person works in, the type of people she works with, and the day-to-day activities that the job entails. Job shadowing also provides an excellent networking opportunity.

Externships

An externship is an extended job shadowing experience that may offer an opportunity for actual hands-on experience as well. Externships usually last from one to five days and often take place during a predetermined block of time.

Part-Time Jobs

Many college students hold part-time jobs, either throughout the entire year or over the summer. These jobs may be on campus or in the outside community. If possible, consider looking for part-time work that is related to a career you might be interested in pursuing.

Volunteering

As with a part-time job, volunteering is a way to get involved in a field of interest for an extended period of time. Volunteering is a great option because it not only gives you the chance to gain experience and insight while contributing to a cause or organization, but also helps you acquire valuable skills for your resume. Furthermore, it's an excellent option for a busy student because you can typically build your own schedule and must only commit to a few hours a week.

Internships

An internship is the most comprehensive form of experiential learning. An internship actually gives you the chance to "test-drive" a career while gaining valuable work experience. As an intern, your duties will typically be similar to those of an entry-level professional and may include a variety of responsibilities and projects. Internships may take place over the summer, during the school year, or may be ongoing. Some internships are paid while others are not, and in some cases, you may be able to earn academic credit as well. An internship can be very helpful in making a decision about a career, regardless of whether the actual experience turns out to be a good one. You may decide that the career is a good fit and pursue it full time upon graduation. Or you may realize that the career is not a good fit at all, and avoid investing time and energy pursuing this option. Finally, as with all of the types of experiential learning we have discussed, an internship can be a very useful networking tool and may even lead to a job offer. Employers often look first to their pool of interns for potential candidates when an entry-level position becomes available. For all of these reasons, completing one or more internships is something all college students should strongly consider.

TED'S INTERNSHIP EXPERIENCE

Ted was a marketing major who wanted to pursue a career in sales upon graduation, though he wasn't sure in what capacity. Ted was also a huge sports fan, so when he came across a summer ticket sales internship with a professional sports organization at his school's annual internship fair, he thought he had found the perfect opportunity

(continued)

to gain sales experience in an area that he was passionate about. Upon beginning his internship, Ted soon realized that while he loved sports, and enjoyed certain aspects of sales, when paired, they were not necessarily a good fit for him. The majority of Ted's days were spent on the phone "cold-calling" potential customers with little to no actual in-person contact—the aspect of sales that he enjoyed the most.

While Ted was disappointed that his internship did not turn out to be all that he had hoped, there was a bright side to the experience. First, Ted was thankful to have realized what he didn't like before pursuing his first full-time job. Second, Ted was exposed to numerous other aspects of a professional sports organization's front office that he had previously been unaware of. One area in particular, the public relations department, especially caught his eye because of the constant contact its employees had with the public. The more Ted learned about the department, the more he realized that it would be a great fit for him—he could have the in-person contact that was missing from his sales position while staying in the field of sports. Ted made helpful contacts within the department throughout the summer and ended up being hired for a full-time position after graduation.

EMPLOYER RESEARCH

So far, we have discussed career research from a fairly broad perspective, focusing on career fields as a whole while briefly touching on employer-specific considerations. In this section, we will narrow our discussion to research strategies and resources that are specific to employers based on their field, as they can vary greatly from sector to sector.

Corporate Employers

When researching corporate employers, start with the organization's website, as well as its annual reports and brochures. Some other especially useful resources are websites developed by Hoover's, Wetfeet, and Vault. These publishers have developed both print and online resources that will help you research broad categories of information about many corporations.

Privately Owned Businesses

Much like researching corporate employers, a place to start when researching a privately owned company is its website, along with annual reports, brochures, and the like. Newspaper and magazine articles as well as the local Chamber of Commerce can also be sources of timely information about a company. Keep in mind that, unlike publicly-owned companies (traded on a stock exchange), private companies are not required to file open public reports about their activities, so tracking down information might be a bit of a challenge.

Nonprofit Employers

Careers with nonprofit employers are an increasingly popular alternative. As you begin to research organizations that you are interested in, utilize their websites and don't be afraid to contact them directly, either by phone or electronically. If you are having a hard time coming up with organizations to research, contact the United Way or another local volunteer network. There are also numerous online resources available for researching nonprofit organizations.

Government Employers

Researching government agencies can be challenging because there is so much information available, and much of it is not centrally located. For the federal government, research the websites of the particular agencies that interest you. You can also personally contact the college relations representative in the federal agency's human resources department to ask about hiring procedures or request additional information. The same process holds true for state and local governments.

International Employers

Two resources (both hard copy and online) that can help you with your search for international employers are the *Directory of Foreign Firms Operating in the United States* and the *Directory of American Firms Operating in Foreign Countries*. These directories, and other online resources, contain contact information for each organization, including mailing address, website, phone number, and email address.

CONCLUSION

You do not need to make a decision about your career right now, but the time and effort you dedicate to researching and experiencing potential careers can greatly enhance the decisions you make in the long run. Furthermore, by understanding how to conduct effective research, you will be better prepared to evaluate the fit between a given career and your Personal Career Profile. Now that you are equipped with the tools for effective major and career research, the next chapter will discuss how to take action.

CHAPTER 8

ACTIVITIES

ACTIVITY 8.1 **IDENTIFYING AND RESEARCHING CAREERS**

Choose two or three careers that you would like to learn more about. Using the various career research resources we have discussed (the *Occupational Outlook Handbook* is a great place to start), consider the following:

1. What type of education or training is required for this career?

2. What is the nature of the work? What daily activities, responsibilities, and projects might a position within this career entail?

3. What salary range can you expect from this career?

4. Are there opportunities for advancement? What are they?

5. What is the employment outlook for this career?

6. How does the career fit (or not fit) with your Personal Career Profile?

ACTIVITY 8.2 **CONDUCT AN INFORMATIONAL INTERVIEW**

Choose a career that you are interested in learning more about. Refer to the guidelines in this chapter to arrange and conduct an Informational Interview with a professional working in that career. Use the list of sample questions (pp. 119–120) as a starting point, but feel free to ask any other questions that you may have.

Reflect on this experience by answering the following questions:

1. Are you still considering this career or a similar one? Why or why not?

2. How did this experience help you in your process of exploring careers?

3. Did this interview answer all of your questions?

4. Do you feel you need more information in order to make an informed decision?

SUMMARY & KEY POINTS

- Your Personal Career Profile (values, skills, interests, and personality) should be considered when deciding what types of careers to research, and also when evaluating specific industries, organizations, and positions.

- When conducting career research, it is important to look at career fields as a whole, as well as specific employers. Knowing where to find this information can make your search more effective and efficient.

- Gaining experience in a given field through informational interviewing, job shadowing, externships, part-time jobs, volunteering, or internships is a vital step in researching potential careers.

MAKING DECISIONS

"Action may not always bring happiness, but there is no happiness without action."

BENJAMIN DISRAELI, BRITISH STATESMAN & AUTHOR

INTRODUCTION

Now that you are equipped with the tools of self-assessment and major and career research, the time has come to put that information to good use and start thinking about your next steps. Making decisions can be difficult; the process may seem overwhelming and potential decisions may seem irreversible. This chapter provides a step-by-step approach that will help you reflect on your current decision-making style and teach you ways to change it, if need be. You'll learn that there is really not one enormous decision you have to make, but rather a series of smaller decisions, each taking you to the next step on your career journey. The truth is that you, and you alone, are the master of your career fate, and taking action is essential to your success.

THE COMPLEXITIES OF DECISION MAKING

When we think of making a decision about a major or a career, it can seem like a daunting task. But, no matter how big or small, decisions are decisions and you are already very experienced in making them. You make decisions all day long, every day of your life. Think of just one trip to a coffee shop: do you order tall or short? Cream or none? Iced or hot? An extra shot, or decaf? Go through the drive-thru or park and go in? We are constantly

Learning Objectives

» Assess your current decision-making style

» Learn to apply a decision-making model to compensate for your decision-making pitfalls and capitalize on your strengths

confronted with decisions, so why do these particular decisions about a major or career consume your thoughts and cause so much anxiety? Realistically speaking, it could be that we know that general happiness in life is positively correlated with career happiness, and most of us have been exposed to people who are miserable because they hate their jobs. And for many people, a job isn't merely a job; it's a fundamental part of their identity and they see themselves only in relationship to what they do (or what they will do). Therefore, people often put a lot of pressure on themselves to do this "right" and make *the* correct decision. But keep in mind that this decision does not necessarily equate with permanence. Remember, the average person will change careers about four times over the course of their working life. You can make adjustments (really just additional decisions) in the future that put you on an entirely different path. Getting a handle on your current approach to decision making, and thinking about how you might improve the process and quality of your decisions, is the best place to begin.

Common Decision-Making Tendencies and Coping Patterns

For any number of reasons, decision making may be a struggle for you even as you enter adulthood. People sometimes unconsciously enlist a series of coping strategies to make the decision-making process feel a bit easier, at least in the moment. While these strategies may make things easier in the short term, their long-term effects can be destructive. See if you recognize yourself in any of the following roles:

- **Impulsive:** you make decisions on the spur of the moment without giving adequate thought to the process of gathering information and considering possibilities.

- **Delaying:** you delay the decision-making process by constant rumination over information or pros and cons.

- **Fatalistic:** you remove yourself from the equation, and leave the "decision" to fate, believing that you are powerless and have little control over the end result.

- **Avoidant:** you avoid thinking about decisions and avoid making any decisions at all.

- **Dependent:** you allow others (parents, friends, faculty members, advisors) to make all the decisions, believing that they probably know better anyway, or perhaps as a way to avoid responsibility altogether.

While these strategies might make things easier in the short term, are they really the best way to make sound decisions? In some cases things might work out fine using these approaches, but in the long term, healthy adults need to develop their own reliable approach to making decisions. Reflect for a moment on your tendencies to rely on one or more of these coping patterns. Do any of them sound like your own decision-making tendencies? If so, think about how you might become more conscious of your reliance on a coping pattern and work to overcome it. Dealing with this may be a challenge for you, but it is certainly one worth confronting. ACTIVITY 9.1 will help you reflect on a decision you have already made, so you can discover a more positive approach for future decisions.

External Barriers to Decision Making

No matter how comfortable we feel about our decision-making process, there will always be obstacles to overcome. Some of these will be imposed on us from outside sources. Sometimes these *external barriers* may simply be the result of the reality of our situation. Sometimes, though, these seemingly external barriers are a result of being externally defined. Remember the discussion of self-authorship in CHAPTER 1? As we become more internally defined, some of these external barriers may dissipate. Do you recognize your own struggle in any of the following scenarios?

- **Family expectations**: Your parents have always wanted you to be a doctor. Since you were born, they told their friends and family that you'd make a great doctor. They told you this, too, as soon as you were old enough to absorb it. They constantly viewed you as the "future doctor" of the family until you began to view yourself this way, too. But now you've discovered that being a doctor doesn't align with your Personal Career Profile, and you decide to pursue a career as a fashion buyer instead. Your family's expectations may be especially difficult to deal with, as you have lived with those expectations for so long. Additionally, your parents may be paying for you to go to school, or you may be conscious of the fact that they have provided for you most of your life. Can you let them down, even if it's the best decision for your future?

- **Expectations of friends or others**: Your friends all came to the same school to pursue a degree in business. You were right there in the midst of it until you began taking courses in the business school and not faring so well. It's not that you can't do the work at the same level your friends can, it's just that you're not motivated to. You've started thinking about other major options but telling your friends will be embarrassing and you might even be disappointing them. They might consider you either a deserter or a failure. Will you be able to break the news to them?

- **Gender stereotypes**: Your culture may view preschool teaching as a typical "woman's job" and chemical engineering as a typical "man's job." If this is the reality of your culture, then it may be a challenge for a man to become a preschool teacher or a woman to become a chemical engineer. Though you may face discrimination and your path to success may be more challenging, will you pursue your dream?

- **Survival needs**: Your Personal Career Profile and career research have led you to the discovery that your dream job is to be a newspaper reporter. You pay attention to the news, however, and you've seen the trend of newspapers dying off. An advisor tells you that this career field is a thing of the past. It seems your need to make a living wage may be in conflict with your career goals. What do you do now?

- **Skill level**: You came to college with your dream already planned out. You wanted to be a nurse. Despite your best efforts, however, in your first semester you got a D in organic chemistry and a C- in anatomy and physiology. The second semester you retook organic chemistry, this time with a new professor and the help of a private tutor. You got a C-. And you took a biology class and got yet another D, though you put many, many hours into studying. The minimum requirements to be accepted into nursing school are quite stringent and you are landing nowhere near them. What do you do now?

Internal Barriers to Decision Making

In addition to barriers from outside sources, *internal barriers* may arise that can challenge your decision-making ability. All of the following barriers arise from within, but that does not lessen their impact on your decision-making process. Think back to the discussion of beliefs in CHAPTER 1. The following barriers may well be rooted in beliefs you currently hold. See if you recognize any of these tendencies in yourself, and if you can identify specific beliefs that might be contributing factors to each of these barriers.

- **Self-esteem**: Your self-worth may be damaged as a result of your childhood or experiences you've had. If you have a tendency to underestimate or devalue your worth, you may be doing undue damage to your career development.

After all, if your opinion of yourself is very low, you are probably not making decisions that will fulfill your dreams. In fact, you may not even be letting yourself dream at all.

- **Self-confidence**: You may lack assurance in your judgment, abilities, or power to influence your situation. If you don't believe your judgment, abilities, or power are sound, you may fall victim to some of the coping mechanisms described previously. Or, if you don't believe in your own abilities or your power to influence your situation, your decisions may not be your own, and that may cause you undue stress and pain as you try to fulfill someone else's vision of what you should do.

- **Fear of failure**: You may have an inherent fear of failure. What if you try to achieve your goals and you do not succeed? The difficulty of that prospect may feel like too much to bear. It may cause decision making to be filled with anxiety, making it difficult to settle on a course of action.

- **Fear of change**: Change might be difficult for you. Perhaps you've always had your mind set on one thing (or others have set it for you), and now you're realizing that a change might be in the works. It takes a lot of courage to change your life's direction.

- **Fear of disappointment**: You may fear disappointing your friends or family, as described previously, but you may also have a fear of disappointing *yourself*. Perhaps you fear that your vision of your future and the reality of your experience may not be one and the same, and you feel stuck. What if the career or major you've envisioned for yourself isn't all it's cracked up to be?

Dealing with Your Barriers

Recognizing your barriers is essential to taking the necessary steps to overcome them (see ACTIVITY 9.2 for help with this process). This part of the process might actually be the most difficult, because it may not be obvious to you what barriers you are facing. Your barriers may impact you from an unconscious level. They may be preventing you from making decisions for reasons that you can't even identify. Your barriers may also be a result of being externally defined. As you progress toward self-authorship, some of these barriers may dissipate, or perhaps disappear entirely. If any of these external or internal barriers to decision making seem familiar to you, or if you're not sure what impedes your ability to make decisions, you might consider career or personal counseling. Your campus career center can assist you with career counseling, and nearly all academic institutions have counseling centers that make personal counseling a viable possibility (both logistically and financially) for students struggling with all kinds of questions, including barriers to decision making. While you may not have considered personal counseling before, in reality many students of both sexes find it quite helpful for addressing everyday problems such as these.

A DECISION-MAKING MODEL

Clearly, the process people go through when making decisions can be complicated. There are many variables and many challenges. Now that you've explored some of these complexities, it may be helpful to examine a decision-making model that can account for some of your decision-making tendencies. Applied intentionally, it can lead you to a better overall process for making decisions.

Think back to the discussion of your personality preferences in Chapter 5. Your personality preferences deeply impact your decision-making style. Knowing and understanding these preferences can help you better understand how you make, struggle to make, or avoid making certain decisions. If you wonder why you have difficulty choosing a major, or if you feel you may have settled on one too quickly, your personality may be a contributing factor. Let's start with a brief recap of personality preferences. Your first preference (Extraversion/Introversion) describes where you get your energy (from external sources or internal sources, respectively). Your second preference (Sensing/Intuition) describes how you take in information (from the concrete environment, or from connections and possibilities you see). Your third preference (Thinking/Feeling) describes how you make decisions once you have gathered information from your Sensing or Intuitive preference. Do you make objective decisions based on a logical sequence of cause and effect (Thinking)? Or do you make decisions based on your values and consideration of subjective influences (Feeling)? And finally, your fourth preference (Judging/Perceiving) describes your need for order and structure in your life.

As discussed in CHAPTER 5, your personality is much more than just four preferences; it is the combination and interaction of your preferences that ultimately describes your patterns of behavior. Refer back to pages 76 and 77 to review your dominant function. Whether it is Sensing, Intuition, Feeling, or Thinking, this is the one that you use most heavily to guide your decision-making processes. The Z-Model is a breakdown of how you might use all four of these factors, in order, as you make decisions.

Z-MODEL

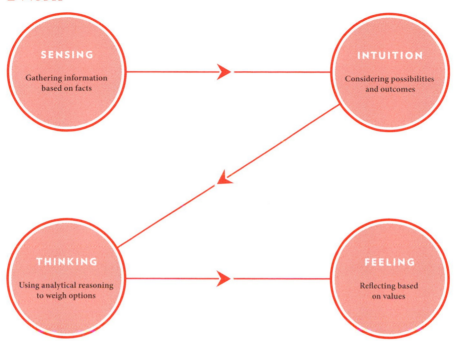

We all use all of these factors as we make decisions, but the theory behind person-ality type suggests that one is your *dominant* function. You rely on your dominant function more than the others when you are making decisions. Remember that it is the captain of your ship. You're more likely to allow your dominant function to guide you because you are more comfortable with it and trust it more than the others. For example, if Thinking is your dominant function, you are likely to spend more time focusing on a logical process than on gathering information, or reflecting. If Sensing is your dominant function, you are likely to spend more time gathering information than focusing on a logical process, or considering possible outcomes. We can break it down hypothetically like this—if you were making a decision that takes roughly 60 minutes to make, this is an estimated breakdown of how you will spend that time:

- **Dominant function:** 28 minutes

- **Auxiliary function:** 18 minutes

- **Tertiary function:** 10 minutes

- **Inferior function:** 4 minutes

As you can see, while your dominant function guides your decision-making process, your inferior function might be neglected. It's worth noting what your inferior function is (pp. 76–77), and how you might make a conscious effort to spend a bit more time with your less preferred functions. If you know your MBTI® type, ACTIVITY 9.3 will help you assess your current decision-making style, and give you the opportunity to exercise your inferior function.

Regardless of which function occupies the majority of your time, your decisions should, and likely already do, incorporate all of these steps (gathering information, considering possibilities, logically deciding, and reflecting on your decision). ACTIVITY 9.4 will offer you the chance to incorporate all of these steps into a career-related decision you are currently trying to make. Becoming familiar with your preferred style and recognizing its potential pitfalls will help you improve both the process and quality of your decisions.

Do You Know What You Need to Know?

No matter how solid your approach to decision making, your decisions are likely to be flawed if you lack adequate information. As we have explored in this text, this information, as related to career decisions, is two-fold: information about self and information about possibilities (majors and careers). If you lack adequate information in either area, any career-related decision you make will be based on insufficient information, making it defective from the start.

You'll always be discovering new information about yourself, as this is a life-long process. But is there more you need to discover *now* about your values, skills, interests, and personality, to make a good decision?

In addition to self-knowledge, you must also have a solid understanding of your options. What majors exist and what requirements exist within them? What careers exist and what are they like? With the hundreds of majors and thousands of careers that exist, it is impossible to know everything about each one. At this point, having a basic understanding of what's available can help you make better decisions about where you might go. Take a moment to think about this. Are you confident you have enough information to proceed? While you don't want to get caught in the trap of continuously gathering information without acting upon it, you also don't want to act prematurely. You can never have *all* the information, but you must have *enough* information.

YOUR BEST-FIT APPROACH TO MAKING DECISIONS

Ultimately, over time, you will discover your best personal approach to making decisions. Be conscious of your tendencies, find your own way, and make an effort to progress toward self-authorship , as discussed in CHAPTER 1. Being realistic is also essential, but try not to let your *perception* of reality cloud your judgment; remember that our perceptions of our world and ourselves are often clouded by our unconscious beliefs. In order to alleviate the impact of your perceptions, gather enough good information from good sources.

SHERRY'S PLANS CHANGE

Since middle school, Sherry had always wanted to be a school counselor. Her encounters with her own school counselor were impactful and in many ways, life-changing. She set her sights on following her dream and was pursuing a course of study that would prepare her well for her chosen career. In order to gain more exposure to the field, and increase the size of her network, Sherry began a series of job shadowing experiences in middle schools and high schools. In her discussions with the counselors and her observation of their work, Sherry discovered that many children were coming from underprivileged backgrounds, and that fact alone was a detriment to their educational success. In fact, as a result of their situations, many kids were not even graduating from high school. One day, a child advocacy lawyer came into the middle school for a meeting with the counselor Sherry was shadowing. As she watched their conversation unfold, Sherry had a sudden realization. Being a child advocacy attorney would allow her to make the difference she was seeking, and do so with children before they even entered the public school system. Though this altered her plans, she remained open to change and began to explore the possibility of a career in law.

Keeping an open mind will also be essential in your career development process. It is crucial to remember that the decision to pursue a specific major or career is really just a series of mini-decisions. You are not permanently bound to the decisions you are making. You can change your mind and you should be open to the prospect of doing so. If you're feeling stuck between two options, try to come up with a third; perhaps there are more options than you realize. You'll continue to make these mini-decisions all your life, because your career development is a process and not a one-time undertaking. Being receptive to change also applies to your own planned career ideal. Though you may have an idea of what you are moving toward, keep an open mind. Acceptance of the ambiguity of this process will be to your benefit. Though this process may clarify an initial direction, it may also give you exposure to new options. Keeping an open mind means being open to change—even if it alters your plans.

CONCLUSION

Making career decisions will likely not be a path without bumps, but making intentional, well-informed, thought-out choices is the surest way for you to achieve success. Keep in mind that your decision-making style can change if you make a conscious effort to improve. With the tools you have acquired in this chapter, you are now better equipped to begin your journey.

CHAPTER 9

ACTIVITIES

ACTIVITY 9.1   **RE-ASSESS YOUR COPING PATTERN**

Think about a time when you have used one of the coping patterns described in this chapter to make a decision. Was it a positive or negative experience? Looking back, what could you have done differently? How can you apply this newfound knowledge to a decision you are currently struggling with?

ACTIVITY 9.2   **DEFINE YOUR PRIMARY BARRIERS**

Which external barrier are you most likely to be impacted by on your career journey? Why?

Now do the same with internal barriers. Which one are you most likely to be impacted by and why?

From these two, choose the barrier you believe will be your biggest challenge and strategize how you might overcome it. What will you need to do to rise above this barrier? How might your perception of the situation, or your beliefs, be influencing your decision making? Do you believe it's possible for you to overcome your primary barrier? Why or why not?

ACTIVITY 9.3   **ASSESS YOUR CURRENT DECISION-MAKING STYLE**

Reflect on your MBTI type, citing your dominant function, as well as your inferior function (see *The Hierarchy of Functions of Each Type* table [pp. 76–77]).

Given your dominant function, what decision-making strengths do you have? Given your inferior function, what challenges might you have in making decisions?

Refer to the list of questions (on the following page) under the heading of your inferior function. How do these differ from the ones you usually ask yourself as you make decisions?

Think of a decision you are currently struggling with. Ask yourself the questions from your inferior function. How does this feel?

Sensing (S)

- How did we get into this situation?
- What are the verifiable facts?
- What exactly is the situation now?
- What has been done and by whom?
- What already exists and works?

Intuition (N)

- What interpretations can be made from the facts?
- What insights and hunches come to mind about this situation?
- What would the possibilities be if there were no restrictions?
- What other directions or fields can be explored?
- What is this problem analogous to?

Thinking (T)

- What are the pros and cons of each alternative?
- What are the logical consequences of the options?
- What are the objective criteria that need to be satisfied?
- What are the costs of each choice?
- What is the most reasonable course of action?

Feeling (F)

- How will the outcome affect the people, the process, and/or the organization?
- What is my personal reaction to each alternative?
- How will others react and respond to the options?
- What are the underlying values involved for each choice?
- Who is committed to carrying out the solution?

ACTIVITY 9.4   **APPLY A DECISION-MAKING MODEL**

Think of a current career-related decision you are trying to make. Answer the following questions about this decision. Try to spend equal time on all four steps.

(1) Gather concrete information:

- Do you have the skills needed for this career?

- How much does this career pay?

- What are the typical working conditions?

- What sources might you use to find out what you still need to know?

(2) Consider possibilities:

- What options exist within this industry?

- Will you be able to use your own unique ideas in this career field?

- Can you create your own job description, or unique role in this career?

- What are your hunches about this career?

- Does this field allow you to adapt and change with the times?

(3) Use analytical reasoning to weigh your options:

- What are the pros of choosing this career?

- What are the cons of choosing this career?

- Will this field provide you with the authority to follow through on your decisions?

- Is pursuing this career a reasonable course of action?

(4) Reflect based on your values:

- How might working in this career impact others you care about?

- How do this career field's overarching goals align with your values?

- Will this decision lead to or maintain harmony?

- What is your personal reaction to this choice? Are you happy about it?

A similar list of questions could be generated for any decision you are trying to make, including choosing a major. Also, note that going through this model once doesn't necessarily mean you'll be ready to make a decision. For example, you might come to reflect on your values and then realize you need to cycle back through to gather additional information. Everyone comes into this process at a different place, spending more time on their preferred functions. The goal is simply to think about incorporating all aspects of this decision-making model.

CHAPTER 9

SUMMARY & KEY POINTS

- Becoming aware of barriers in your decision-making process will help you overcome them and move forward.

- Understanding your current decision-making style can open your eyes to its pitfalls and allow you to use some of your less-preferred tendencies in order to make better decisions.

- By applying a decision-making model, you can make more informed, better thought-out decisions.

CHAPTER 10

SETTING GOALS

"To reach a port, we must sail—sail, not tie at anchor—sail, not drift."

FRANKLIN ROOSEVELT, 32ND PRESIDENT OF THE UNITED STATES

INTRODUCTION

As you begin to make decisions about your future, you may start to feel more confident and more secure. In fact, it may be such a relief that you will want to react by taking it easy for a while. But it will take more than deciding on a career to make your dreams become reality. Say you decide that you want to pursue a career as a physical therapist. You feel confident that this career choice is a great match for your Personal Career Profile, and you decide you want to pursue this path with all your heart. If you hope for it and cross your fingers it will happen for you, right? You'll wake up in a few years with a great gig as a well-paid physical therapist. Well, of course, hoping that your future will be secure and fulfilling is a natural human tendency, and there is nothing wrong with that. But for your dream to become reality, hope must be accompanied by some tangible action on your part. So, as you begin to make decisions about your future, it is wise to begin thinking about setting concrete goals for yourself. What's next? How will you know if you're on track? What if you lose your way? Goal setting will help you answer these questions and make necessary adjustments along the way, much like adjusting to changing winds and sailing with intentionality toward a destination.

Learning Objectives

» Understand the importance of setting goals

» Learn methods to make your goals more achievable

PERSONALITY AND GOAL SETTING

Just as your personality preferences impact your decision-making process, they also impact your goal-setting process. At the most basic level, the last letter of your personality type will tell you a lot about your method of setting goals. Those with a preference for Judging (J) tend to like closure and will thus maintain a rather structured approach to their goals. They often enjoy the idea of moving through a plan, as they find it satisfying to accomplish tasks, and an open-ended approach might feel stressful. But those with a preference for Perceiving (P) may prefer a more open-ended approach, and may find highly-structured plans to be too confining. Your preference for Judging or Perceiving can make the process of planning and goal setting either more or less comfortable for you. Being aware of your tendencies is always the first step. The next step is to try to keep from falling into a trap due to your personality preferences. For those with a Judging preference, this might mean keeping an open mind about other options and trying to approach goals with some flexibility so that a change of course is possible when it is necessary. For those with a Perceiving preference, this might mean keeping some structure to your approach, so as not to lose track of your goals altogether.

LEVELS OF GOALS

Thinking of "goals" in a generic sense can throw your brain into overload fairly quickly. Instead, think of your goals in levels—some are your highest, overarching goals. These meta-goals will encompass the big picture of your life. What are the broadest concepts that motivate all aspects of your life? It might be helpful to think about the discussion of values in CHAPTER 2, as well as the mission statement you wrote in CHAPTER 6. What are the universal values you chose? Perhaps these are principles such as safety, self-sufficiency, power, self-expression, or balance. These are what motivate you from within and what you are ultimately striving for in your life. ACTIVITY 10.1 will give you a chance to reflect on your mission statement and visualize it playing out in your life.

At the next level, you'll have more specific goals that will support your meta-goals, as well as your mission. These will be more tangible and will be steps toward achievement of your meta-goals. For example, if self-expression is a meta-goal, specific goals that support that might be writing in your journal, painting, or engaging in relationships in which you are free to express yourself fully. Or, perhaps your specific goal might be pursuing a career in an environment that will support your self-expression, such as the arts, or writing, or higher education.

Once you have an idea of some specific goals, you will be able to formulate the most tangible goals—action steps. Action steps are the things you need to do to accomplish your specific goals (which in turn support your meta-goals). Returning to the previous example, if your specific goal is to pursue a career in writing, one action step might be to conduct three informational interviews with individuals who work for online magazines. The remainder of this section will focus on the last two types of goals (specific goals and action steps). Remember, though, starting with meta-goals and working backward is the most logical way to set goals that are tangible enough to achieve. Always keeping your meta-goals—as well as your larger mission—in mind is important, and you should constantly consider what they are and evaluate whether your current specific goals and action steps are supporting them.

SMART GOALS

One way to assess your goals is to consider whether they are SMART—that is whether they meet the criteria defined by that acronym (adapted from the SMART System developed by Kenneth Blanchard and Spencer Johnson):

- **Specific:** Is your goal specific enough so that you will know when you have accomplished it? A generic goal is not nearly as powerful as a specific one. For example, planning to "talk to people about a political science major" is not nearly as specific as "I will talk to one student majoring in political science, one political science advisor, and one political science professor about the major."

- **Measurable:** Is your goal tangible enough that you can measure it effectively? For example, hoping to "improve my GPA next year" is not nearly as powerful as "planning to improve my GPA from 3.1 to 3.4 by the end of the next academic year."

- **Attractive:** Is your goal appealing to you? This may seem like a silly question, but take a moment to reflect upon your goal. Is it truly *your* goal? Or does it belong to someone else (a parent, a friend, a teacher)? Achievement of your own goals can be difficult enough; achievement of someone else's can be miserable, and can certainly become a barrier to your success. In order to have the tenacity to fulfill a goal, it must be attractive to *you*.

- **Realistic:** Is this goal feasible for you? This, too, may seem like a silly question, but if you're setting goals that are unrealistic, you are not likely to accomplish them. Think about your goal with this mindset for a moment. Some people actually advocate for setting goals outside of your reach (and thus might seem "unrealistic"). Doing this might help stretch your potential, but it also might disappoint you if you don't succeed. Ultimately, you know yourself better than anyone else knows you, so you will have to be the judge of what a "realistic" goal looks like for you.

- **Time-bound:** Does your goal have a time frame? If not, you may still be working toward it in 50 years. Give your goals specific time frames so you will be able to stay on track and move forward to another goal in a reasonable amount of time (for example, "getting an internship in an art museum," vs. "getting an internship in an art museum the summer between sophomore and junior year"). If you stick with the time-bound goal, you're more likely to achieve it within a reasonable time frame.

Making sure your goals are SMART is an effective way to make sure they are achievable. ACTIVITY 10.2 will help you assess one of your goals by these criteria to see if it's SMART.

Write Them Down!

Accountability for your goals is a proven factor in making them more likely to come to fruition. One form of accountability is simply to write down your goals. Having goals in your mind is one thing; having them on paper is quite another. Writing down your goals is like creating a contract with yourself. A study conducted by Dominican University proved that participants who were held accountable for their goals were more likely to follow through on taking steps to achieve them. Additionally, those who wrote down their goals (rather than committing only mentally, or verbally telling someone else) were much more likely to actually achieve their goals. Therefore consider writing down your goals for the day, week, year, or for your life. Place them in an area where you will encounter them often, and hold yourself accountable, just as you would another party who entered into a written contract with you. Try this strategy by completing ACTIVITY 10.3.

Prioritization and Flexibility

Not all of your goals will carry the same level of importance or urgency. You may need to act upon some today, while for others you may wait until tomorrow, next week, or next year. Prioritize your goals. What do you need to act upon now? What can wait until next semester? What should wait until next year? Prioritizing is not always easy. Sometimes it's helpful to discuss your goals with someone else in order to help you determine their urgency. If you think this would be helpful for you, share a few of your goals with a friend, advisor, or professor, and seek their opinion on the best way to approach them.

In addition to prioritzing your goals, being flexible is also invaluable. You will certainly encounter roadblocks along the way to achieving your goals (ACTIVITY 10.4 will help you identify possible roadblocks, as well as strengths). Life doesn't always happen as we think it will. In fact, it rarely does! Being able to adjust and alter your goals as roadblocks occur will be essential. This may be as simple as reprioritizing your goals or it may be as dramatic as changing your major, or working toward an entirely different career goal. Even though adjustments may be difficult, being open to new information (about yourself and about the possibilities that await you in terms of majors and careers), and being flexible in your approach to your career development will benefit you in the long run. Always consider whether you are still truly working toward your meta-goals.

CONCLUSION

Visualize, prioritize, and write down your goals sooner rather than later. Begin making conscious choices, and allow yourself the freedom to change your mind along the way. This will allow you to guide your own career fate, and make your dreams reality.

CHAPTER 10
ACTIVITIES

ACTIVITY 10.1 **VISUALIZE YOUR MISSION IN ACTION**

1. State again (or revise) your Mission Statement from your draft (p. 101).

2. Visualize: How might your mission statement look in each part of your life?

- **Right Now: Doing It.** How does my mission statement connect to what I'm doing right now with school, community, family, and friends?

- **Short Term Goals: Deciding.** How does my mission statement connect to where I see myself going in the next year with my major, career, and extracurricular options?

- **Long Term Goals: Dreaming.** How does my mission statement connect to how I see my life 10 years from now (family, lifestyle, community)?

ACTIVITY 10.2 **SMARTen YOUR GOALS**

Choose one goal you are currently working toward and assess it for SMART-ness. Write down the goal and then write down each element of a SMART goal (Specific, Measurable, Attractive, Realistic, and Time-bound). How does your goal match up to each of these five criteria? What can you do to make your goal SMARTer?

Write your goal here: _____

_____

S _____

M _____

A _____

R _____

T _____

ACTIVITY 10.3   **CREATE WRITTEN GOALS**

Write down a goal you hope to achieve for yourself within the next three days. It can be anything at all (e.g. finishing your biology paper, making your car payment, running two miles, reorganizing your closet, calling a friend back home). Tape the written goal to your door so you'll see it every time you leave your room, and create a screensaver with scrolling text that directly states your goal. After the three days are up, reflect on the following:

- Did you accomplish the goal?
- Why or why not?
- What did it feel like to be constantly confronted with your goal?
- Would you change anything the next time around to make sure your goal becomes a reality?

ACTIVITY 10.4   **CONDUCT A SELF-SWOT ANALYSIS**

A SWOT analysis is an evaluation of strengths, weaknesses, opportunities, and threats and is often used by organizations to strategically plan for the organization's future. Try one on yourself, using your career planning process as your backdrop. Analyze your strengths, weaknesses, opportunities, and threats (as related to your career planning process) by writing down all the factors that come to mind in each area.

As you work to identify strengths and weaknesses, it may help to think back to the previous discussions in the textbook dealing with self-knowledge, including beliefs, skills, personality traits, and internal barriers. As you work to identify opportunities and threats, consider people you know, your environment, economic conditions, opportunities and experiences you may have been (or may be) exposed to, and external barriers.

Strengths
What attributes do you possess that will help you achieve your goals?

Weaknesses
What attributes do you possess that might become obstacles in your pursuit of your goals?

Opportunities
What are some external conditions that exist for you that might help you achieve your goals?

Threats
What are some external conditions that might become obstacles in your pursuit of your goals?

After you have determined your strengths, weaknesses, opportunities, and threats, consider how you might make use of this information as you move forward and set goals for yourself. For each strength you listed, write down one way you can capitalize on it. For every weakness you listed, write down one way you can improve upon it. For every opportunity you listed, write down one way you can make the best use of it. And for every threat you listed, write down one way you may be able to minimize its impact.

Now, consider this self-analysis in its entirety. What impact might it have on your ability to reach your goals?

Revisit this activity often on your journey; each component will likely change as time progresses. This exercise can help you keep a realistic view of your situation, and strategize about how to capitalize on your strong points and compensate for your weaker ones in order to achieve your goals.

CHAPTER 10

SUMMARY & KEY POINTS

- Setting goals is crucial to achieving career success.

- Making your goals specific, measurable, attractive, realistic, and time-bound will make them achievable.

- Creating a realistic implementation plan for your goals includes knowing your strengths and limitations, and understanding the importance of prioritization and flexibility.

MAKE YOURSELF MARKETABLE

"The only source of knowledge is experience."

ALBERT EINSTEIN, PHYSICIST

INTRODUCTION

Once you set goals, the next step is to start thinking about what you need to do to achieve them. How will you make yourself marketable to potential employers in your field of interest? What will set you apart from your peers? How can you prove your skills to potential employers? Addressing these questions early is the surest way to make your dream career become a reality. This chapter will introduce you to the concept of gaining experience and marketing yourself in order to achieve your goals.

WHERE TO BEGIN

All the knowledge of self, career options, decision making, and goal setting in the world will not get you very far if you're not able to secure employment. Now that you've had a chance to reflect on your decision-making process and think about setting goals for yourself, your next step will be to consider how you will represent yourself to potential employers. It may seem like this is not something you need to devote any attention to just yet, but it will be most effective to work slowly and steadily toward the accumulation of marketable skills. After all, it takes time to build new skills. Think about the following questions. What skills do employers seek in qualified candidates? What skills do you

Learning Objectives

» Recognize the impact that marketable skills can have upon your job search

» Discover how to gain valuable experiences while you are in college

currently possess and want to use? What must you do to obtain the skills you need to succeed? How can you prove to potential employers that you have these skills?

MEETING EMPLOYERS' NEEDS

Your potential employers will be in search of various skills, depending upon your chosen career field. Think back to the discussion of skills in CHAPTER 3. Remember the difference between transferable skills and specialized knowledge? The specialized sets of knowledge that employers seek will always be dependent upon the field. Transferable skills, however, are applicable across fields. Employers from all different fields report some basic transferable skills and personal attributes that they seek in employees. These include:

- communication skills
- teamwork skills
- motivation and initiative
- interpersonal skills
- strong work ethic

- analytical skills
- flexibility and adaptability
- computer skills
- attention to detail
- organizational skills

If you were an employer, wouldn't you want your employees to possess these skills and attributes? In order to make yourself marketable, you should acquire as many of these skills as possible and practice them often, so they will be perfected and easy to prove to a potential employer in the future. You also need to be aware of the specialized sets of knowledge required by your chosen career field. Your work here will be two-fold: determine the skills you will need, and assess the skills that you currently have. Think about what gaps you see, and work to fill them by building new skills over the next few years.

Building Skills

You can't do much to change your personality, even if you wanted to. You also can't force yourself to be interested in something that you don't care about. And, while they may change over time, your values are not something you would usually wish to compromise. Skills, however, are changeable. You can adjust them, learn them, practice them, and perfect them as necessary.

THE VALUE OF EXPERIENCE

Josie was a fantastic student in the classroom. She attended class every day, always completed her homework assignments, studied hard, and aced nearly every test she ever took. She graduated from her university with a 3.8/4.0 GPA, and then began her job search. As she began to think about creating a resume to apply for jobs, she realized that she did not have anything to put on it besides her degree, which filled up only about five lines, leaving a vast empty space on the page. As she looked at that empty page, she could not understand how she had let this happen. She was a smart young woman and she knew she was capable of anything. But how could she prove it? Her short, unimpressive resume did not reflect her capabilities. Employers would certainly be impressed with her high GPA, but would want to see more experience. Josie ended up taking an unpaid internship after she graduated. Because it was unpaid, she didn't have enough money to support herself. She ended up moving back home with her parents and taking a part-time job as a server to make her college loan payments. After one year at her internship, she felt that she had enough solid experience to prove her skills to other employers, and she began her job search anew; she finally landed an entry-level position, more than one year later than her peers.

Academic institutions offer you the chance to build a number of skills without ever leaving campus. First, your education itself is designed to enhance your skill set. Remember the discussion of majors in CHAPTER 6? Do you ever wonder why you must take general education courses that don't seem to relate directly to your major? Those courses are designed to provide you with a well-rounded education, building skills and a greater understanding of the world. Immerse yourself in your academic work. Make class attendance a top priority and participate in discussions. Get to know your professors by arriving early, staying late, and visiting during their office hours. Your classroom experiences can provide you with ample skills (e.g., writing, presenting, critical thinking) and specialized knowledge, but you must take a proactive approach to get the most out of them.

In addition to your education inside the classroom, you can take advantage of your free time by using it wisely to build the skills you need to succeed. You've already learned how to use extracurricular experiences as research tools; now consider them as factors influencing your marketability. Think about the following options:

- **Part-time jobs**: Obtaining a part-time job either on or off campus will give you real-world work experience. Don't underestimate the marketability of part-time work. It gives potential employers insight into your work ethic and your time management abilities, and you learn transferable skills at the same time. Often, students who have part-time jobs perform as well or even better than their peers academically. Sometimes you can even receive financial aid by working part-time. Your academic institution likely has a mechanism to help you search for part-time jobs. Start with a visit to your campus career center to learn more about your school's process.

- **Campus activities**: Campus organizations provide an easy access route to developing new skills. Greek organizations, student government, and other student clubs and organizations provide opportunities to build skills in organization, time management, and leadership, to name a few. Make the most of each activity you're involved in by becoming a leader in a limited number of activities, rather than joining multiple organizations just for the sake of joining. Being a "member" in a dozen organizations is not nearly as valuable as being the president of just one. Volunteer to join committees and take active leadership roles to gain valuable skills. Your school likely has a student activities office; visit it early on to see what opportunities exist.

- **Volunteering**: Volunteer experiences can also help you build skills while contributing to a cause you believe in. Just because these experiences are unpaid does not diminish their value. On the contrary, employers understand the benefits of volunteering, and are likely to appreciate a citizen who is willing to give back to their community. Many campus organizations provide opportunities to volunteer in the community. Your student activities office can help you locate such groups. For opportunities to volunteer on your own, check to see if your community has a local volunteer network, or contact your local United Way.

- **Internships, Externships, and Job Shadowing**: Few things substitute for being in the environment you want to work in. What better way is there to decide if you really want to do a job than to try it out? Internships, externships, and job shadowing allow you to do just that. Along with being in the environment, you will also gain experience and expand your network. Most students complete at least two internships by the time they graduate; be proactive and seek out these opportunities early on so you don't fall behind your peers. It's never too early to start; the summer after freshman year is a great time to do an internship. Many internships (though not all) are even paid. Visit your campus career center early in your college experience to learn more about these opportunities, including where and how to find experiences that will best support your goals.

- **Study Abroad:** International experience is very marketable in today's global job market. Studying abroad can help you build skills in languages and contribute to your knowledge of diverse people and other cultures. Your college years are a convenient time in your life to immerse yourself in another culture and live abroad for a few months. Your school likely has an office designed to help you obtain information on studying abroad. Contact them early so you can plan your education around such an experience.

Proving Your Skills

You can say you are a good communicator or leader, but how can you *prove* it? You will have to do this eventually in your resumes, cover letters, portfolios, and interviews, but it will make that task much easier if you think of these things as you go. Portfolios, for example, are collections of tangible evidence of your skills. As you progress through your college career, collect these tangible pieces of evidence, also known as *artifacts*. For example, you may wish to prove your marketing skills by showing potential employers an advertisement you designed for an event you planned. Or you may wish to prove your skills in written communication by displaying a letter you wrote to solicit donations for your volunteer organization. ACTIVITY 11.1 will help you get in the mindset of proving your skills by thinking about your portfolio as it is now, and as it might be in the future.

It will also be helpful for you to build a resume and prepare for interviews, since both of these activities require you to prove your skill set to potential employers. Writing down your skills and experiences as you accumulate them will be much easier than trying to remember them years from now. Visit your campus career center to get started. For comprehensive information about the job and internship search, see the companion to this text: *Ready or Not: The Art & Science of the Job Search*.

NETWORKING

In addition to building skills and knowledge while you are in college, it is also essential to establish and expand your list of personal contacts. "Networking" is really just building relationships by exchanging information. As you learned in the context of career research, networking through informational interviews is a great way to learn more about careers. It is also a terrific way to increase your marketability. Employers typically prefer to hire people through referrals or from within the organization, so most job openings are never advertised anywhere. Your ability to access this invisible job market, therefore, depends on people. As you gain experience as described previously, talk to the people you come in contact with. Get to know them and maintain those relationships, even after you move on from a particular part-time job, internship or other experience. When it comes time to search for jobs, you will have a better idea of what's available, and you will also have many people who will be glad to testify to your skills by serving as references or writing letters of recommendation. And remember, your ability to give back to your network will expand as you grow professionally; networking is a two-way street.

CONCLUSION

As you acquire experiences, you will be increasing your marketability and learning a great deal about yourself in the process. Make note of your peak experiences, as well as those that feel uncomfortable or unenjoyable. Using the tools you have gained from this text, try to discover what it is about an experience that you like or don't like. This ongoing discovery of self-knowledge will help you immensely as you continue to cycle through the career development process.

This text has equipped you with tools to increase your knowledge and awareness, both about yourself and about the world of work. Remember that the career journey is just that, a journey. It is not a destination, as the career development cycle will continue for the rest of your life. So, get ready for what will literally be the ride of your life. Enjoy the journey!

CHAPTER 11

ACTIVITIES

PLAN YOUR PORTFOLIO

Visualize your portfolio as it looks right now.

- What are three to four artifacts you could include to prove your skills?

- What are three to four skills you wish to develop?

- What artifacts do you need to attain in order to prove your skills?

- How might you attain them?

CHAPTER 11

SUMMARY & KEY POINTS

- Employers seek candidates with specific skills, which can be gained or enhanced through experience.

- You can obtain and perfect many of the skills you need to succeed through extracurricular activities and part-time work while in school.

REFERENCES

- Baxter Magolda, M. (2001). *Making their own way: Narratives for transforming higher education to promote self-development.* Sterling, VA: Stylus.

- Ben Franklin, *Wit and wisdom.* Accessed October, 2009, at http://www.pbs.org/benfranklin/l3_wit_self.html.

- Briggs Myers, I., McCaulley, M.H., Quenk, N.L., & Hammer, A.L. (1998, 2003). *MBTI Manual: A guide to the development and use of the Myers-Briggs Type Indicator® (3rd ed.).* Mountain View, CA: CPP, Inc.

- Briggs Myers, I., Kirby, L.K., & Myers, K.D. (Ed.). (1998). *Introduction to type: A guide to understanding your results on the Myers-Briggs Type Indicator® (6th ed.).* Mountain View, CA: CPP, Inc.

- Brown, D. (1995). A values-based approach to facilitating career transitions. *Career Development Quarterly,* 44(1), 4–11.

- Donnay, D.A.C., Morris, M.L., Schaubhut, N.A., & Thompson, R.C. (2005). *Strong Interest Inventory manual: Research, development, and strategies for interpretation (Rev. ed.).* Mountain View, CA: CPP, Inc.

- Grossman, J., Hanvey, D., Kreitl, B., Lloyd, K., Van Dyke, J., Paley, L., Podsiadlik, N. (2009). *Ready or not: The art and science of the job search.* Bloomington, IN: Career Development Center and Arts & Sciences Career Services.

- Holland, J.L. (1992). *Making vocational choices: A theory of vocational personalities and work environments (2nd ed.).* Odessa, FL: Psychological Assessment Resources.

- Martin, C. (1997). *The dynamic basis for type.* Accessed March 22, 2010, at http://www.capt.org/mbti-assessment/type-dynamics.htm. Center for the Application of Psychological Type.

- Maslow, A. (1954). *Motivation and personality.* New York, New York: Harper & Row Publishers, Inc.

- Myers, K.D., & Kirby, L.K. (1994). *Introduction to type dynamics and development: Exploring the next level of type.* Mountain View, CA: CPP, Inc.

- Zunker, V. (2008). *Career, work and mental health: Integrating career and personal counseling* (pp. 15-36). Sage Publications: Thousand Oaks, CA.